PRAISE FOR LIFE ACCORDING TO PERFECT

Bestselling author and speaker Ralph Harris knows what it is like to hurt and what it means to trust Jesus. Here, Ralph creatively shares with us the importance of the indwelling Christ, illustrating in clear ways how we can know Jesus as our everything. Whether your struggle is fear or faithfulness, "Life According to Perfect" will encourage you in ways that only few books do. Get this book to find real answers and discover real healing.

Dr. Andrew Farley, best-selling author of *The Naked Gospel*, and host of "Andrew Farley LIVE" on Sirius XM

Captivated from page one, my imagination dropped right into the setting of this delightful story, *Life According to Perfect*. What I didn't expect was the lump in my throat that got bigger and bigger as the story unfolded. "This is my life with Jesus," I thought, "How could someone else describe it so well?" By the last page, the lump in my throat burst into an explosion of joy. All I could think was, "Oh, how I love Jesus…"

Tricia Gunn, author of *Unveiling Jesus* and

founder of Parresia

One of the things I like most about Ralph Harris is that he is exceedingly funny and sharp, but Christ in him has caused him to be safe, sincere and real. So he gets to offer us a story that is profound, simple, innocent and delightful—all at once! *Life According to Perfect* is an unusually engaging, enjoyable and important book, because it pictures beautifully the God of all grace, as well as what He is like in those He inhabits. Enjoy!

John Lynch, Trueface, author of *On My Worst Day*, and co-author of *The Cure*, *Bo's Café*, and *Behind the Mask*

Life According to Perfect is a delightful invitation to journey into the very heart of God. This Godly allegory gracefully and powerfully gives words to the rhythm of intimately walking with God in ways I have never read before. I was entirely captivated, and took notes for myself about the deep wisdom revealed in the relationships found in this story. It's outstanding.

Tracy Levinson, best selling author of *Unashamed - candid conversations about dating, love, nakedness & faith*

So many people settle for the false security that following fear promises and miss out on the exhilarating joy and freedom that perfect love provides. In this beautiful story, my good friend, Ralph Harris, in his uniquely simple yet profound way, brings down to earth, right where we live, the heavenly reality of God's love and presence and shows us the practical and transforming way of grace. You will be inspired and excited as you read *Life According to Perfect*, knowing that you are loved!

Tim Chalas, Lead Pastor at Grace Life Fellowship, Baton Rouge, Louisiana

I wish there were more stories like this gem, written by Ralph Harris. *Life According to Perfect* gives a vivid portrayal of the shared life that Christ offers to all. It brilliantly illustrates the joy of walking in the Spirit, and the freedom of choosing to be who God made you to be. If you are done with fear and shame, thrill to the words of the One who says, "I am Perfect, so you don't have to be."

Paul Ellis, author of *Stuff Jesus Never Said*

This book, *Life According to Perfect*, declares in a fresh, disarming, non-religious way the biggest issue I have found in every human I have met or tried to help; a need to be related to based on their value not their behavior. That's what John 3:16 states, and my friend Ralph Harris communicates it with as much passion and precision as anyone I know.

Dean Sherman, Traveling Teacher with Youth With A Mission (YWAM) since 1967

I felt that God was a master manipulator in the sky just waiting for me to come around a corner so He could drop a piano on my head, while thinking, "What can I do to punish Kelsea next time?" In *Life According to Perfect*, Ralph writes in a way that hit me right between my eyes and deep in my soul about how simply and easily God loves me and wants to be with me through all the little goings-on in my life. This story, deeply profound and stunningly simple, re-ignited a fire in my soul that God is FOR ME, and He is my constant cheerleader, confidant and friend. This is a must read for all ages, but particularly those who have felt that God is somehow against them—or just not FOR them. But He is, and He wants to know YOU. There is no better book than this one to prove it to you.

Kelsea Maynard, El Segundo, California

Nobody tells the story of God's love for humanity better than Ralph Harris. *Life According to Perfect* is a unique and creative tale in which you will experience the true heart of God come alive to your senses, and it may just change your life forever! Get, read and give this book away! You will be glad you did.

Jeremy White, Pastor, speaker, and author of *The Gospel Uncut: Learning to Rest in the Grace of God*

Ralph lays out a story in *Life According to Perfect* that you will be quickly absorbed in, and then gives wonderful theological truths minus the jargon. His story tells the truth about our journey in a world of chaos, and how living out of proper identity helps orient us in the world and spreads light in the darkness.

Paul White, author of *Revelation to Transformation*

Ralph Harris is a modern-day C.S. Lewis! *Life According to Perfect* opened up my heart and mind to who, what and where I always am in a way I never dreamed possible. Equally important, it revealed how fear exposed loses its power and control, and I'm deeply grateful for that. I've put in my first order for 50 copies!

Bradley Harris, Senior Director, Multinational Customers/Deutsche Post DHL (Retired)

I couldn't put this book down! Now I can't get the truth of it out of my mind! In *Life According to Perfect*, Ralph Harris uses the medium of a story in the same way as the Master Story Teller, Jesus, did. You become part of the story as you see yourself in different characters. Next, you are faced with the vastness of fear's control. Finally, your entire being rejoices and relaxes as the hero emerges in a most unlikely manner to liberate you.

Mark Maulding, author of *God's Best-Kept Secret*, and President of
Grace Life International

I haven't read a book I've liked this much in the last 10 years.
Wonderfully conceived, wonderfully told, and brilliantly simple.
Just like Jesus.

David Gregory, author of New York Times' best-seller, *Dinner With
A Perfect Stranger*, and *The Rest of the Gospel*

I just read Ralph Harris' refreshing fable for the soul, *Life According
to Perfect*. Ralph spins a tale that seems to come from the experience of every person who has ever lived, and beckons each of us to
the deep, intimate fellowship of journeying with the lover of our
soul as our closest friend. Get this book, because not only will it
bring sweet revelation of God's love, but you may well realize this
story is your story.

Mike Q. Daniel, speaker, writer, and ministry coach
at ZoeCode.org

In our journey through what can be a dark and lonely world, if you
listen, you can hear the heart cry of every human being: "Is there
anyone out there who will care for me? Is there anyone out there
who will love me? Is there anyone out there who will fight for me?"
In this wonderful story, *Life According to Perfect*, Ralph Harris
answers those questions with a resounding "Yes" as He introduces
us to the Person of Grace – Jesus! Get this book and devour it, and
allow the power of this story to lead your own heart into the safe
and loving arms of the One Who loves us so dearly.

Frank Friedman, Teaching Pastor at Grace Life Fellowship, Baton
Rouge, Louisiana

LIFE ACCORDING TO PERFECT

THE GREATEST STORY NEVER IMAGINED

RALPH HARRIS

CONTENTS

To the greatest loves and co-laborers of my life, wife Sarah, and daughters Ellen and Emma. My heart is engaged and full because of you.

～

Thank you, David Gregory, for helping me to write more clearly what was in my heart. You are a true friend.

～

Thank you, Phyllis Harris, for so beautifully translating the wonder of this story to the cover of the book.

1

ELLIOT

Elliot didn't like chickens. He liked eggs all right, but chickens themselves were mean and cruel and jerky, and they were never happy. Have you ever seen one smile? No. Elliot stayed away from them—until he couldn't.

"Elliot! Elllll-iiiiiiii-oooottt!" his mother called. "I want you to take some eggs over to Mrs. Boyer's. We owe her for the vegetables your father brought home two nights ago. Take six."

"Mom!" he protested.

"Do as I say, Elliot Benjamin," his mother, Hannah, ordered. Elliot didn't have to see his mother's face to know she wasn't giving him any options. When she used his middle name, it meant he responded immediately, like a soldier when ordered by his captain. Anything less meant punishment.

"Yes, ma'am," he uttered, and began moving toward the barn.

He hated chickens.

Elliot thought that one day the mangy birds would ambush him for stealing their eggs, and that his lifeless body would be found near the chicken coop with 473 holes in his head. He imagined his parents would cry, and that the neighbors would gather around and wring their hands in lament. Maybe then they would see how dangerous and evil chickens were and banish them forever, eggs or no eggs.

But not today.

With a dejected sigh, he pulled on the thick leather gloves hanging in the barn, grabbed the padded egg basket, and made his way to the chicken house. Elliot knew the birds would hate him all the more because the usual time for egg thievery was before dawn. Then the wicked creatures were asleep, and he suffered only an occasional peck. This was an unusual raid, and he knew he'd have to look under most all of the squatting and squawking birds before finding enough eggs. This would be war.

He drew in a last breath of fresh air and threw open the door to the hen house.

Bad Bart, king of the coop, jerked his chicken head at Elliot and blasted a loud cackle-shriek, sounding the chicken alarm. Immediately, chaos erupted. Elliot, waving his free arm in self-defense and to inflict a little pain on the attacking birds, moved forward to claim his treasure. One egg here, another there, he slowly made his way from nest to nest, smacking at squawking and defiant hens while enduring their savage pecks.

When at last he'd snatched enough, Elliot carefully backed his way toward the door, lifted the latch, and lunged through the opening. Only after slamming the door shut on the screaming hen house did he let down his guard. "I hate chickens," he muttered.

Gathering himself, he brushed off the chicken war evidence and called to his mother. "Mom, can I take Harvey?"

A slow, massive horse, Harvey was perpetually filthy—and lazy. He spent most mornings rolling in the mud by the water trough, which, Elliot suspected, was his method of avoiding work. It was very successful. Only when his father needed him in the spring to plow the fields did anyone dare get close enough to wash and brush the smelly beast. But, dirty though he was, a ride on Harvey to Mrs. Boyer's was better than a walk.

"No, Elliot," his mother replied, "you know you can't ride alone, and your father won't be back from the shop until after dark. Get going."

Elliot's father owned a leather shop in Sarx, the small town nearby. People from miles around gave him their business, but that didn't mean they willingly paid for it. Many times Elliot had watched people's faces contort in protest and their fists clench when the bill was presented, even though they'd agreed to the cost to begin with. "Why, you're a thief, Frank Samuelson!" they'd shout. "I've half a mind to never come back here again! I suppose you're training that son of yours to rob us too!" And there were fights, ugly and awful. Although Elliot helped out only on weekends, he saw enough to know that his father was tough and strong and unyielding all the time.

"Elliot," he'd say, "people will take you for all you've got every chance they've got. You've gotta be ready for 'em! That's why I'm making a man outta you—so you'll be ready to take over here when the time comes."

It seemed to Elliot that his father spent as much time arguing and fighting with customers as he did working with leather. Because he worked long hours, he wasn't home very much, which meant limits for what Elliot could do—like ride Harvey. Though he was only twelve, Elliot knew he could handle the big horse on his own. But not today. Dejected, he put the gloves back in the barn and headed for the trail that led to Mrs. Boyer.

The woods around Sarx were dense and dark. Briar bushes and willows tangled the forest floor, and passing through meant a difficult slog around buggy bogs and over sharp rocks that jabbed at him menacingly.

As Elliot worked his way to the top of the first hill, pushing through the bushes, he paused for a moment. Pine and oak trees tangled the sky, but he could just make out three plumes of smoke from Sarx. One was from Mr. Ferrin's blacksmith shop, one was from the town's little market, and one plume of smoke was from his father's leather shop. Often on warm days like this, his father would make glue from leftover scraps of leather. The smell was awful, and no one went near the shop on glue-making days. Elliot wondered if his father didn't make glue with the sole purpose of driving people away. It sure worked when he got home. There would be angry words and a lot of loud and frustrated stomping after he came through the door.

Pushing on, Elliot reached a small clearing through which he could just make out the roof and chimney on Mrs. Boyer's still distant house. As he walked, cradling the egg basket in his right arm, the sense that someone was watching him entered his mind. "There's no one here," he argued aloud. "No one ever walks in these woods." Yet the feeling persisted, and when he thought he heard hoofbeats, he whirled around.

"Is someone there?" he asked. Elliot wasn't afraid, but he couldn't shake the feeling that someone was near.

Still, there was nothing.

"Strange," murmured Elliot, as he turned again toward Mrs. Boyer's house. Soon, he reached the low stone wall surrounding the Boyer property, climbed over it, and strode the path leading to the door. Before he could knock, the door flew open and Mrs. Boyer, disheveled as ever, was waving a hefty cane at him.

"What are you doing on my land, boy? Have you come to steal? Is that it?"

"No, no, Mrs. Boyer!" Elliot hastily replied. "I'm Elliot Samuelson, and I'm here with some eggs."

Still holding the cane threateningly over her head, Mrs. Boyer sneered. "Well, it's about time one of you good-for-nothing Samuelsons paid me back. When was it your father came begging anyway? A week ago, wasn't it?" Finally, she lowered her weapon.

"It was just two nights ago, and we're thankful to you," Elliot said.

"Well, you should be," she hissed, hastily taking the eggs into her apron. And without so much as a goodbye, Mrs. Boyer took a step backward into her house and, sneer fixed upon her face, slammed the door shut. Elliot could easily hear through the door her final words to him: "Now get off my land! Be gone, Samuelson!"

2

MUD

The next day dawned cloudy and wet, though Elliot wouldn't know it until he climbed out of the dingy cellar where he slept. He could always get more sleep there because his parents' bickering couldn't be heard as easily through the thick floor. It had become his haven.

After climbing the stairs, he realized the day was getting on because neither his father nor mother was present. Elliot would be in some trouble since he was supposed to walk to school. Why had he overslept? Why hadn't they wakened him? After a piece of bread, some cheese and milk, Elliot hurried out the door to make his way to town.

The path to Sarx was a muddy mess since it had rained most of the night. Elliot was glad, however, that for now the rain had stopped. He detested arriving at school looking and smelling like a wet mop, mostly because the town's kids were merciless and would launch their taunts at the slightest opportunity. To be prepared, Elliot often practiced a perfectly vicious response to silence his critics. There were lots of fights, and he wanted to be ready to defend himself, whether verbally or physically.

Navigating the less muddy places on the path, Elliot recalled the day when, right in front of the whole school, Greg Ragsdale made fun of him. "Hey, scarecrow boy! Does your father make you stand in the garden after school? How many crows did you scare away yesterday?"

It was true that Elliot was thinner than the other boys, and that some of the pants he wore were too short, exposing his skinny legs and clunky shoes. That day he'd given Greg a punch to his stomach, and when he doubled over in pain, Elliot jeered, "What's wrong, Greg? Got a stomachache? Or maybe you're just religious and bowing down to me! I think I like it."

The good feeling of winning that day returned to Elliot, and, nodding in self-congratulations, he said aloud, "It'll be a long time before Greg Ragsdale messes with me again. If ever he does, I'll. . ."

Just then Elliot was drawn out of his thoughts by the sudden awareness that he was being watched, just like yesterday on his way to Mrs. Boyer's. He quickened his pace. Eyes darting ahead and behind, he could find nothing to explain his sense that he was not alone. He was certain, however, that he could hear the hoofbeats of a horse. And wasn't that a whinny? Why couldn't he see it? In an instant, Elliot broke into a wild dash along the path, suddenly convinced that running to town was his best choice.

The oozing mud, like the disgusting glue his father made, flew up at him, collecting on his pants and coat and slowing him down. Still, Elliot reached the edge of town, where he hoped someone might see him and come to his rescue. Feeling safer, he slowed and risked a look behind. There was nothing. There was no one.

Puzzled and breathing heavily, Elliot rounded the corner of the town's store and bumped right into Nancy Eaton. "Oh, no!" he thought.

"Oww!" Nancy exclaimed. "What's wrong with you, Elliot? Why, you're all covered in mud! You look like a pig! You're more of a pig than you are a scarecrow! Ha, ha! Scarecrow's become a pig."

Nancy Eaton was at least as mean as Greg Ragsdale, maybe more so. Her whole family had mouths as wicked as whips. No one in town could match their ability to criticize, but because three of them were in school, Elliot couldn't avoid them. Unfortunately, he couldn't out-insult them either.

"Look, I'm sorry, Nancy," offered Elliot, "I didn't see you there."

Nancy's face turned even more sour. "Is that supposed to make it better, Pig Boy? You've got mud all over me. Wait 'til I tell my brothers—they'll get you for this!"

The Eaton brothers were the dread of the town—at least for those who were school aged. Most everyone else just put up with them because their parents were the loudest and most obnoxious people in the world. Whenever you met any of them, you soon felt like their role in life was to punish people. Even if you had done nothing wrong, they would cook up something in their head and begin prosecuting their case against you. Elliot thought the whole family was a walking death sentence.

"I said 'I'm sorry,'" replied Elliot.

"Well, that's not good enough, Samuelson," Nancy replied with a jeer. "I think you'll have to pay for ruining my clothes. You owe me two dollars, Samuelson! Pay up, or I'll tell Tad and Tom right now!"

Elliot didn't have fifty cents, let alone two dollars. "Um, I . . ." he stammered, fully intimidated. "I'll have to owe you. I, I can get it to you next week. Just give me until next week, will you?" he pleaded. Elliot had no idea how he could get that much money, but putting off an immediate beating was his immediate goal.

9

"Well, you'd better do it, Samuelson," Nancy scolded, "or Tad and Tom will tear your arms off."

As she turned and stormed off, Elliot muttered a little too loudly, "Gee, I suppose that would hurt."

Nancy spun around and yelled, "That's three dollars now, Samuelson! I heard what you said! You hear me?! Three dollars!"

"Okay, okay. Three dollars! Just don't tell your brothers."

As Nancy stormed off, he thought, "What kind of a day is this, anyway? And I haven't even gotten to school yet."

Elliot was a muddy mess. Never had he been so embarrassingly filthy, and he was sure to hear all about it when he got to school. What would he say? How would he explain his appearance? He couldn't tell everyone that he had been running from something invisible; that would sound crazy. He'd have to make something up. Maybe he was muddy because a bear came at him from out of the woods, or a mountain lion and he was just able to escape. There were lions around Sarx, and sometimes people were attacked. Think of the terror. Or maybe he had to avoid a sudden rockslide that almost swallowed him up. "It might work," he said aloud as he imagined the faces of the listening school kids. "Hmm. This could actually be good for me."

Happily lost in a fantasy world where he was becoming more courageous and heroic by the moment, Elliot failed to see a horse and rider crossing the road just in front of him. Stumbling from the jarring collision, he fell backward to the ground.

"Hey!" barked Elliot, "Watch where you're going, mister!" Elliot looked up to see the rider, but the sun above and behind the figure prevented Elliot from making out his features.

"Ha, ha," chuckled the rider, "I *was* watching where I was going, Elliot."

Squinting and shielding his eyes from the blinding sun, Elliot tried to see more clearly.

And then the horse and rider vanished.

3

SCHOOL

S tartled, Elliot picked himself up and quickly searched all around. Nothing. The horse and rider, as suddenly as they had appeared, were gone in an instant. How could that be? Was he mistaken? Had it been his imagination? That couldn't be. There were hoof prints right in front of him. Trying to remember what he had seen, Elliot realized that but for the nearly blinding light, he had seen very little that he could easily describe.

And how did the rider know his name? Elliot was certain he had seen enough to know that he didn't recognize the man, yet the stranger spoke his name.

Standing puzzled in the middle of the road, Elliot was distressed to hear the schoolhouse bell. He was late. He shook his head to clear his mind and began to run the short distance to school. Happily, Elliot saw that he was not the only one late for school; Don Nibecker was running from the opposite direction with a wild look on his face. As everyone knew, their teacher, Miss Breckett, was terribly positive, and the shame she heaped upon the last student to arrive after the tardy bell was positively unbearable. It was a sprint for classroom survival.

"You'll be sorry if you get there before I do, Samuelson!" Don Nibecker screamed a warning.

Undaunted and running for his life, Elliot reached out his hand for the latch on the closed schoolhouse door as he drew near. He was going to win! As he closed his hand on the latch, Don bashed into him from behind, throwing both of them into the closed door. Legs and arms tangled from the collision, Elliot and Don crashed to the ground. Before either could recover, the door flew open and Miss Breckett stood over them glowering.

"Well, Mr. Sameulson! And Mr. Nibecker!" she all-too-happily exclaimed. "While I'm delighted to see you both, I must inform you that you're not exactly on time for school. Please disentangle yourselves—gently now, Mr. Nibecker! I'm quite certain Mr. Samuelson does not enjoy your elbow at his throat."

The only good thing about Don Nibecker was that he was not big enough to be a genuine bully. However, it seemed to Elliot that it was nevertheless Don's highest aspiration in life: Don Nibecker— Bully Supreme. That he was outclassed by the Eaton boys, Tad and Tom, didn't slow him down or disillusion him in the least. He didn't have the brawn of the Eatons, but he tried to make up for it with cunning and sharp elbows. His bully tactics were strategic and nearly constant. He'd push you out of line, throw water on you, put a tack on your chair, and elbow you in the ribs when Miss Breckett wasn't looking. He'd steal your lunch and begin eating it before you knew it was missing, and then for no apparent reason, he'd get your attention and flash a mouth-full-of-food grin at you. When the revelation struck you as to what Nibecker was eating—your lunch —Don's face would positively radiate with glee. *Gulp!*

If ever there was a person related to a wolverine, Don Nibecker was it, thought Elliot.

"Get offah me, Nibecker!" Elliot bellowed.

"You're the trouble, Samuelson!" yelled Don. "You tried to cut me off at the door!" And, appealing to Miss Breckett, Don pointed his boney hand at Elliot and shouted, "He was last! Samuelson should be punished, Miss Breckett!"

With an overly bright smile erected upon her face, Miss Breckett snatched Elliot and Don by their shirt collars and maneuvered them into the classroom. Wild cheering erupted immediately. "Now, now class," Miss Breckett intoned happily. "We mustn't ridicule Mr. Samuelson and Mr. Nibecker too harshly. After all, they're well aware that a penalty awaits them." How she could make impending doom sound like a happy song, Elliot could not fathom, but there it was.

Miss Breckett fancied herself as heaven's own sunbeam. She radiated such unwavering happiness that virtually everyone else was a shadow to be transformed by her sparkling brilliance. Or vanquished. Once, when Elisabeth Barger's dog, Baxter, had been run over and killed by Mr. Nelson's wagon right in front of the school, Miss Breckett insisted that it was actually a good and happy moment. Taking Elisabeth's face in her hands, she magically smiled a brilliant smile, and insistently sun-beamed both horror and sorrow out of the moment. "Now, boys and girls, I'm sure God needed Baxter in heaven with Him," she beamed. "Let's just think of all the angels enjoying Baxter right now! Can you imagine him running and jumping and licking their angel faces? Why, I wonder how big Baxter's wings are, don't you? Can you see him flying with the angels? Of course you can! Come now, children, let's go to class."

And without so much as a "Goodbye, Baxter," Miss Breckett herded the class into school. Everyone disliked her, but had to pretend they didn't. After all, how does someone contend with overwhelming sunshine?

"Let's all sit down now, students," she said joyfully, "and we will decide what the penalty shall be for Mr. Samuelson and Mr. Nibecker." "We" never actually meant *we*, as in the entire class having something to say about it. It meant that Miss Breckett was exacting punishment *through* everyone, as if *we* had all become part of the humiliation she was pouring out upon darkness.

"We know they meant to be at school promptly—certainly we do!" she said. "So let's have them write on the chalkboard, 'I am a prompt person, and promise to always be prompt at school, at home, and in all of life.' Isn't that wonderful, children? Isn't it just right?" she exclaimed. "And let's have them each write it—oh, twenty times. Yes, twenty times, Mr. Samuelson and Mr. Nibecker, while we watch."

The last three words of the punishment were the ones most hated —". . .*while we watch.*" Each punishment pronounced ended with the same words. In truth, everyone feared Miss Breckett, even while she commanded postured affection. She ruled with a smile in a way that made all of the children her prisoners. Elliot wondered if one day the punishment would be to give himself twenty lashes with a horse whip, while standing in front of the class. Control would be absolute if she could get her students to punish themselves whenever needed. Then maybe the classroom would be sunny.

But not really.

4
—————

LUNCH

His hands still dry and chalky, Elliot fussed with the mud caked on his coat as he slunk outside for lunch break. There would be none for him since he'd had to rush out the door earlier in the morning without taking time to prepare a lunch. His meager breakfast would have to sustain him through the day.

"Hey, pig boy! Did you bring some corn from the pig pen for lunch?" Donna Jensen and Stacey Hawkins, two of the loudest-mouthed, most sarcastic kids imaginable, scanned Elliot's area for food. Together, they were a bothersome gang. Obviously, Nancy Eaton had been spreading her new nickname for Elliot.

Summoning his defensive skills, Elliot said, "Why yes, I did! I've been saving some for my piggy friends!" he snorted. "Here, let me help you feel like home. Let me give you a hug!"

As Elliot walked toward the girls and reached out his muddy arms, their faces registered shock and they quickly withdrew saying, "Get away, Samuelson, or we'll tell Miss Breckett on you!"

"Really? Are you sure you don't want a hug?" sneered Elliot. "We could sit together in the puddle by the shed," he offered. To his relief, Jensen and Hawkins hurried away, leaving him alone.

"What a day!" he muttered.

His thoughts returned to the events of the morning, including the mysterious run-in with the stranger on horseback. Who was that? Had the stranger been following Elliot? Was that whom he'd run from on the road to town? Elliot suddenly recalled the odd sounds and sensation he'd had while on his way to deliver eggs to Mrs. Boyer the day before. "Why is this happening to me?" he wondered. "Is anyone else aware that there's a stranger in town?"

Just then Emile Finch walked past, and Elliot asked, "Hey, Finch! Have you seen any strangers in town lately?"

"No way." Emile replied. "Why would anyone come to this town anyway?"

"Well, uh, have you felt at all like you were maybe being watched recently? Like someone you couldn't see was watching you?" asked Elliot cautiously.

"What's wrong with you, Samuelson? Has the pigpen affected your brain? What there is of it. . ." Emile said as he walked away, laughing.

At that very moment, Elliot felt again the odd sensation of being watched. He glanced about the schoolyard in search of someone studying him. No one was. In fact, all of the other kids and one or two adults who were monitoring them were engrossed in what was right in front of them: the schoolyard rope swing, the hole Matt Dilhoffer was digging, and an argument that pitted Dan Westerly against the Eaton gang. *That* was sure to be fun.

Still the feeling persisted, and it was becoming clear to Elliot that he was the only one aware that there was someone watching, someone that seemed just out of sight and unknown.

The ringing school bell interrupted Elliot's thinking, calling him back inside. Sally Moran was pulling the bell rope for all she was worth, which most everyone thought wasn't very much. She was all arms and legs, and fairly groaned her way though life, including now as she worked the rope. "Ehhhhh! Ughhhhh! Ehhhhh! Ughhhhh!" she cried. Miss Breckett had awarded the position of Bell Ringer to Sally at the beginning of the school year as though it was the most sought after honor one could possibly achieve. It became her title: Ringer of the Bell. Occasionally she would bestow the temporary honor upon a lesser classmate, making sure the so-honored paid due respect by thanking her profusely. But as soon as the event was over, each one chosen returned to calling her the nickname Dan Westerly had bestowed upon her: *Dingbat.*

Actually, she *was* a dingbat, or so Elliot thought. No one could ever talk with her without Sally launching into a string of complaints about how bad life was. Listening to her was unbearable. And really, no one thought she had much of anything to be upset about. She often wore new clothes, had better lunches than everyone else, and never walked to school because her father delivered her each day by wagon. What was so bad? No one knew, but most decided to go along with it and make her life worse by calling her names. "Dingbat" was just the latest. Former names included Sourpuss, Chicken Butt (Elliot's favorite), and Corky, because one day Dan Westerly got so fed up with Sally's complaining that, although he meant to say, *"Can you just put a cork in it?!"* he instead blurted out, *"Corky!"*

Elliot regarded Dan Westerly as the town nuisance. At all times, Dan made you feel badly by criticizing anything and everything he could think of. He'd tell you that you were stupid, that your nose was too long or too fat, your teeth were crooked, your feet too big, and your ears too long. It was as if he was everyone's evil mirror, reflecting back their worst suspicions about how they looked. He was a walking plague of hurt and sat right next to Elliot in class.

The only good thing about it all was that he often fumbled his words and said something entirely confusing in the midst of being critical. "Samuelson," he once said angrily, "I hate you so much I'm going to face your smash!" Dan didn't seem to appreciate it when Elliot, at first cowering in fear, burst out laughing. Although Dan got the words mixed up, he straightened them out on Elliot's face.

But Elliot wasn't powerless, nor was he a coward. He was careful to avoid conflict when possible or when he thought he would lose, but when necessary, Elliot stood his ground. He was particularly good with words, and could use his fists if needed—like when Westerly or Nibecker or an Eaton boy picked on him.

Fighting one's way through conflict was the way of life in Sarx. Everyone had a nasty edge about them that cut into everything. Even holidays, such as they were in Sarx, were famous for fights that broke up families and ended friendships. The only way that anyone ever had dinner at someone else's home or ever got together for Christmas or for a birthday was either you were new in town (and it was rare that anyone moved to Sarx), or the inviter hoped to make an alliance with you against someone else. It was a team-building kind of thing, a way of mustering strength for when you had to go against an enemy.

Even Reverend Fortner, the town's lone clergyman, was the epitome of managing the town through conflict. It wasn't that he would necessarily *cause* the problem; he'd simply point out *who* the problem was. Through the magnifying glass of his sermons, each week Pastor Fortner would rail about something that made God mad. It might have been smoking or drinking or not tithing or swearing or kissing in public or showing up late on Sunday. And always his messages were so fiery and clear that everyone knew someone who was, in fact, making God consider bringing Armageddon early to Sarx. Though most of the town didn't go to Reverend Fortner's little church on Sunday, everyone knew by sundown who the offender of the week was. Under pressure from the little congregation, either the offender confessed the error of his ways publicly and promised to behave, or he became the target of gossip and rumor . . . and Reverend Fortner's pulpit prayers on Sundays. Even God couldn't help him then.

"Almighty God, we know that you are a perfect God, who visits perfectly upon us what our deeds deserve. Not one of us escapes your view, not one! Not even Mr. _____, who ignores your merciful command to repent and who defiles this land. Ohhhh, God! Let not his transgressions be visited upon us. Spare us and bring him to church that he might repent and escape the fires of hell. Amen, and amen."

Secretly, Elliot wished that God would make Reverend Fortner and Miss Breckett get married to each other. He gleefully imagined the fights they would have struggling for power—Pastor Fortner, snarling and jabbing his finger in the air, and Miss Breckett, smiling and sun-beaming her way through the darkness of their home.

Secretly, Elliot wished he lived somewhere else.

5

FIRE

"Mr. Samuelson," Miss Breckett called, "What do you think?" Elliot had no idea what she had been talking about, so he had little chance of giving the right answer.

"Um, please, Miss Breckett, would you repeat the question?" he asked.

Ravishing in radiance, Miss Breckett replied, "I am certain that you, along with the class, were paying attention, Mr. Samuelson. Why would you need me to repeat the question I know you've already heard?" The only time laughter was permitted in the classroom was when someone was being scorched by Miss Breckett. It seemed to assist her.

But this time a classmate unintentionally broke up the beating.

"There's smoke coming from the church! Fire at the church!" shouted Ruth Simpson.

Everyone rushed to the window where they could see smoke billowing from the rooftop and steeple. Even Miss Breckett could not restrain her students as they stormed the door and flooded onto the road that led to the church.

As Elliot ran up the road toward the church, he saw Reverend Fortner in front waving his arms and shouting. It crossed Elliot's mind that the reverend really didn't look much more animated than usual. At least now he had a reason.

The town's volunteer fire department, which included Elliot's father, arrived just moments before Elliot and the rest of the school. Three of the men began working furiously to get water out of the pumper tank and onto the growing fire. Everyone was yelling and screaming about what to do, and, except for the firemen, it was mostly chaos. Mr. Atkins finally unhitched the fire department's horses from the pumper tank wagon, risking his life to coax the frightened and rearing animals away from the flames to safety. It was a wonder he wasn't kicked.

Reverend Fortner, still waving his arms and shouting, attempted to direct everyone as if he knew what he was doing. "Put your backs into it, men; you're in the service of the Lord! Push back these flames of hell! Hurry, men!" All but a few ignored him.

Mercifully, Jim Talt yelled: "For God's sake, man! Get out of the way, we're trying to save you!" Still, if it weren't for Mrs. Westerly urging him away, Sarx might have been out of a reverend that night.

Mr. and Mrs. Westerly had come to Sarx some thirty years before, looking for a place to settle down and raise a family. The two of them practically built the little store all by themselves. Dan came along several years later, and about a year after that, Mrs. Westerly announced that she was expecting their second child. Tragically, Mr. Westerly was killed when he fell from Randolph Cliff while hunting, and Mrs. Westerly miscarried. She never remarried, but devoted herself to the task of running the store. It was as if she got lost in it, because no one saw her at any events or gatherings or at the school for her son. Everyone knew her scales were fair, and if you special ordered something, she always made sure you got it. But no one got anything extra. There was no credit, no layaway, no sampling the candy, no loitering, and no laughter in the store. She was stern without being cruel, but the difference was subtle.

Reverend Fortner reluctantly backed away, exactly as Mrs. Westerly had commanded.

At about the time when it seemed that the church building wouldn't survive, Elliot got that feeling again, like someone was watching him. He glanced about, searching for someone he didn't recognize, but only in a half-hearted way. After the events of the past two days, Elliot didn't really expect to see a stranger amongst the crowd gazing at the burning building. Right then he was surprised to discover that, while everyone else was fairly frantic and worried, he was strangely calm. Elliot alone knew there was a stranger amongst them, and he alone was peaceful, as though the presence of the unseen stranger somehow reassured him. That was odd.

"Elliot! Elliot!" his father shouted.

"Yes, sir?" answered Elliot. His father, drenched in sweat and covered with ashes, had momentarily walked away from the war on the fire.

"Elliot," he asked, taking him firmly by the arm, "did you have something to do with this fire? You or anyone you know?"

"No, sir! I had nothing to do with it," Elliot said quickly. He was saddened that his father had even asked him such a question.

"You're sure?" asked his father, staring intensely into Elliot's eyes. Much of the town disliked the church, but it startled Elliot to think someone might have set the blaze on purpose.

"I know nothing about it, father," replied Elliot. The best answer to his father's questions was always the shortest and most direct.

"Alright then. See that you tell me if you hear anything. I've got to go now." His father turned and marched back to the battle for the church.

In the moment following, Elliot blinked and blinked again. He was used to being questioned by his father, but this? Wiping the tears from his eyes, he felt the same aching sorrow he'd had many times before. In a little bit, Elliot would cover it up, at least on his face. But he knew again that no one, not even his father, really knew him or believed in him. Oh, his mother and father *said* they believed and trusted him, but when something bad happened, they talked to him in a way that revealed they really didn't. This was just one more time.

With the men of the fire department working feverishly, there wasn't much anyone else could do except stay out of their way and watch the church burn. And it did. Everyone said the men weren't to blame; there was simply no stopping it. But no one was hurt, and they kept it from spreading to anything else.

A couple of hours after the fire began, it was all over. "Okay then," Elliot said, and he turned toward home.

6

PERFECT

The trail around Burro Hill presented a more desirable way home, so Elliot took the turn past Mr. Ferrin's shop. Except for a few horses in the corral, it was unusual that the blacksmith's barn was deserted this time of day—but this was an altogether unusual day.

There had once been a crude road at the base of Burro Hill, but the heaviest spring rain anyone could remember had swollen the river and washed out the old bridge. The story was that besides Luke Dornan, who raised burros and pastured them on the far side of the Buffalo River, only one or two people ever used it. Mr. Dornan demanded that money be raised for the rebuilding of the bridge, but because no one saw the need like he did, it never got done.

Perhaps a year after the flood, Mr. Dornan failed to make the most precarious turn on another road as he traveled home from a town meeting. Some say he was crazy-drunk, but in any case, his wagon rolled over on him and he was killed. Though it wasn't official, that dangerous turn in the road became known as Dornan's Corner. You had to go slowly if you and your wagon were going to make it.

But Elliot loved Dornan's Corner. While it was steep, you could see the entire valley and beyond from it. And if you did it just right, you could run full speed down the hillside, taking care to avoid stumbling, and leap into the river at the bottom. Elliot thought a wild sprint and dunk in the river was just what he needed to get the day off his mind.

"Ready! Set! Go!" shouted Elliot, launching himself. "Woo-hoo!" He bounced and nearly flew through the air as he dashed down the hill. "Woo-hooooo!" The final part was Elliot's favorite. A massive slab of rock provided a ramp from which he could hurl himself out through the air, then to crash into the deep pool below. "Woo-hoo!" he yelled, flying off the rock which jutted out over the river.

Even though it was late August, the water in the Buffalo was always icy. Elliot plunged far over his head into the pool, drawing a closed-mouth "Ooooh!" from him that meant both distress and delight. Kicking to the surface, he yelled with all his might as he bobbed into the air. "Woo-hooooo!" It was the most exhilarating thing he knew.

Elliot began swimming to the far side of the river, now wanting to get out of the frigid water as fast as he could. He always wondered after the plunge just why he did it. "I've gotta be crazy!" Elliot exclaimed. "It's freezing!" But he loved it.

When he was able to touch bottom, he began picking his way through the rock-filled shallows, which was the worst part of swimming in the river. The Buffalo had lots of sandy parts in it, but this wasn't one of them. His feet always took a beating climbing out of the water, slipping and pinching between the smooth rocks the size of round loaves of bread, making his shoes almost worthless. "Dang!" he yelped, and "Daaang!" again.

Finally, he reached dry land, where he rolled onto his back to dry off in the warm, late afternoon sunlight. Stretching out, he closed his eyes and murmured, "Ahh. Just what I needed."

He was being watched again, he knew. While the realization made him more alert than he might otherwise have been, Elliot wasn't afraid. He couldn't explain why not; he simply didn't feel threatened.

After a while, Elliot knew he'd better get moving or he might not get home with time enough for his chores. Harvey was due to be combed, curried and fed, and his stall cleaned out, and the chickens would have to be gathered and ushered into their house. It was far less of a battle to get them in for the night as it was to capture their eggs. They seemed to know that the dark of night meant danger from coyotes, barn owls, and the occasional bobcat, so they strolled willingly to the safety they knew well. Elliot was careful to count them each evening so as to be certain that none were left outside. Death would be virtually certain otherwise.

Wet shoes squishing, he began walking the faint trail home, which he alone knew about, since he'd made it himself. Only in a few areas could one be certain of the trail, which Elliot mostly navigated with the help of certain recognizable trees and rock formations. Sut's Hollow, a small clearing that briefly interrupted the otherwise dense forest, was just before him. From early spring and deep into summer, bright and showy wildflowers flourished here, but were mostly gone now as summer turned to fall.

In the fading light of the afternoon, Elliot abruptly stopped. Just before him, where a small spring trickled out from beneath a great old pine tree, a huge and noble elk paused to drink. Though he was mere feet from the magnificent animal, it showed no fear of Elliot. The elk slowly raised its antlered head from the narrow ribbon of water as if to get a better look at Elliot, but quickly resumed drinking after sizing him up.

"Why isn't he afraid of me?" thought Elliot. Bull elk always bolt and rush away at the smallest sign that people are nearby, yet this one remained. Sut's Hollow seemed like the safest place on earth, and Elliot was captivated by the overwhelming tranquility he felt. Obviously, the elk felt it too.

Taking it all in, he became aware that the light of day was changing. It wasn't that it was diminishing so much as the light seemed to be moving. While trees and earth remained stationary, the sky itself was gathering from all around and collecting just to the left of the elk. Light was becoming something else, something drawn together and tangible before Elliot's eyes. He stood still, transfixed. The elk was also watching, unafraid that anything threatening was occurring.

Soon it was evident that the light was forming into a horse and rider. "Wow!" said Elliot, "maybe this is my stranger."

Immediately came a reply that Elliot felt more than heard, and which filled the hollow. *"I am!"*

Elliot drew back in response. His mind immediately suggested running for home because he should be afraid. But somehow, he wasn't.

Shortly he could see a white stallion, powerful and spirited, yet content to be managed by his rider. Elliot was sure the animal was prepared to do anything at any moment should his rider decide. He was stunning and fearsome. The rider, Elliot could see, was tall, valiant and imposing in the saddle, every bit as capable as the horse beneath him indicated. He was clothed in fine garments and protective leather, and Elliot had no doubt that the man could effectively wield the long sword in the scabbard at his side. Together the two conveyed invincibility.

Elliot was trembling.

"Fear not," the rider said, but Elliot couldn't help shaking in awe just a bit as the man began to turn his face toward him. In the instant their eyes met, fear fled. It didn't vanish, thought Elliot; it didn't disappear. It felt like fear, craven, cowering and suddenly exposed, ran out of Elliot, clamoring and protesting as it did. Elliot gasped and it was gone.

His eyes wide and body trembling in wonder, Elliot stammered, "Who ... who are you? What have you done?"

"Are you bothered?" asked the man.

And in that moment, Elliot realized the man's face and all of his demeanor was lit with bright joy. He was the happiest man Elliot had ever seen or could imagine, for that matter, as if he didn't have a single thing to worry about because he knew everything was all right.

Astonished, Elliot had nothing to say. Recognizing Elliot's awed silence, the stranger laughed a deep and comforting laugh that filled the hollow, and said, "Yes, I am happy! And I am happy for you to meet me, Elliot Samuelson."

"But how can you know my name?" asked a bewildered Elliot. "And who are you? How did you get here?"

The man replied, "Let's start with my name; I am Perfect. What do you think of that, Elliot?"

"Well," Elliot said, "something is sure different about you, I'll say that. But how'd you get that name, 'Perfect?'"

The man answered with confidence and pleasure. "I'm here for you to know, as many have before you. I will show you why I bear this name."

7

FREEDOM

Still guarded, Elliot kept his distance. The bright light that had come from everywhere to form the horse and rider had now faded completely. If he hadn't seen it with his own eyes, Elliot would think of them now as a normal. But he *had* seen their transformation; of that he was sure. But not much else made any kind of sense.

Elliot decided to show the man that he was nobody's fool and no one to challenge. He was long practiced in defending himself with words.

"Look, um, *Perfect*," he blurted, sounding tough. "I don't know what's going on, but let me tell you that . . ."

"Whoa, whoa, young Elliot," interrupted the man, raising a gloved hand. "It is understandable that you are afraid of me. You've never seen anyone like me." He laughed. "And rightly so, for there is no one at all like me. But I am kind and good, as you will see."

"I'm not exactly afraid of you, Mister," replied Elliot, neglecting to use the man's name.

"And why not?" the stranger asked, smiling.

"Well, I was, I was afraid. I mean, who wouldn't be, the way you showed up and all. But when you looked at me, I felt something happen, something *inside*. I felt fear leave me. Did you do that?"

"In a way," said the man, his face aglow with delight. "I am the opposite of fear, and it cannot remain where I am. It is of no effort from me that fear departs; it simply must, so it did." His face seemed to warm Elliot's heart. "What do you think of that, Elliot?"

It struck Elliot that both the man and the horse were now looking at him intently, as though they were cheerfully anticipating his answer. Maybe they knew it already. Just to the right at the spring, the elk was also calmly staring at him, as though it too was awaiting his reply.

"I don't know what to think," said Elliot. His eyes filled with tears and he was trembling again. "Ever since yesterday when I think you were following me—you were, weren't you?" Elliot asked. When the man nodded, he continued. "Something strange has been happening to me. I don't know if I knew what fear really was, or how big it is. But now that it's gone. . ." He paused for a moment to think, and then continued. "Whenever I thought you were near and watching, I felt as though I waited for fear or looked for it to move me—*I expected it*—but it wasn't the same. It didn't do it. Does that make sense? Is that fear?"

"It is," the man said.

Elliot saw that the stranger's eyes were also filled with tears, which sparkled and spilled down his joyful cheeks.

"How do you feel without fear?" the man asked.

"I—I don't know!" Elliot replied. "I think I've always had it, so I'm not sure what to do without it. Wasn't it me? Won't I need it?"

"Ho-ho, no!" laughed the man, and the hollow was filled with the happy sound. "Fear strangles people and twists them, making them less than they really are. It is one of my chief delights that they are free of fear with me. People become more than ever what they really are."

"Well," said Elliot, taking a step toward the man and horse, "I'm not at all sure what to expect around you, but I feel better than I ever have. And didn't you say that you're the opposite of fear? What are you then?"

The horse immediately rose-up on its hind legs, carrying the man with it. It shook its head and whinnied a short blast of a whinny. As horse and rider returned to the ground, the man grinned mightily and said, "Yes, yes! He always does that when someone asks who or what I am. It delights him so." Drawing a great breath, he exhaled and asked, "Who do you think I am, Elliot? What would you say after our meeting today?"

"I, um, I don't know," Elliot stammered.

"Very well," the man replied, nodding and grinning again. "I'm glad you've not decided. I am especially happy that you don't think I am your enemy. That's good, Elliot," he said, "There's no hurry about me, and we'll meet again soon enough. That I know."

"Are you going to keep following me?" Elliot questioned.

Chuckling, the man replied, "Would you mind if I followed you? Would that be so bad?"

Elliot rubbed his forehead and answered, "Well, no. I don't suppose it would. But will you be, um, invisible again?"

"What do you think, Elliot?"

"I think invisible is mostly how you are, since no one else has seen you," Elliot replied. "And why does no one else see you? Why only me?"

With a great and shining smile, and eyes that conveyed a happy and secret knowing, the man answered, "That's a good question, Elliot. I have deeply enjoyed our meeting. I will see you soon."

And with that, the horse shook its head and whinnied, and began moving toward the forest. "Until then!" the man said, in a voice that filled the hollow. And before Elliot could blurt out the questions pouring through his mind ("When will that be? Where?"), the horse and rider glowed brightly for a moment and vanished.

"How does he do that?" Elliot asked aloud.

An unexpected response thundered and shook the hollow: "Woo-hoooooo!" Birds burst from the trees and scattered excitedly into the evening sky, and not even the elk, which bolted into the surrounding woods, remained calm. To Elliot, it seemed even the trees were waving their arms in recognition of what had just happened.

"Well, I never," murmured Elliot.

Standing in the absence, he realized that he was not the least bit certain of what had just happened. "Now what?" he thought. "How do I just go home? What do I say?" Quickly, he decided to get moving. The walk home would perhaps give him enough time to figure out what to do. Still, how could he tell anyone what had happened? They would surely think he'd lost his mind or was lying, and for that he would be punished, something Elliot knew all about.

8
FEAR

P unishment. Elliot dreaded it.

As he began walking for home, he remembered the most recent punishment his father had given him. Coming home late one night from the shop, his father slammed the front door and tromped down the stairs to the cellar where Elliot was reading by candlelight. His father rarely sought him out except to tell him what chore had to be done or how he'd failed. Elliot could tell by the sound of his father's heavy feet on the stairs that this time he'd done something wrong.

Everything inside of Elliot tightened.

"Elliot!" his father said harshly, before he had made it all the way down. "You left the gate open on the pigpen this morning, and Harvey's been rolling in it all day. How many times have I told you to close that gate?! How many? Why don't you ever get it right?"

Elliot, who had quickly gotten to his feet in his father's presence, was careful to look at him when he spoke. It was an awful torture to watch the angry displeasure on his father's face, but failure to make eye contact during one of these chewing-out sessions was a sure avenue to a worse outcome. No matter what, it was going to be bad anyway.

"I'm sorry, father," Elliot offered. "I don't know why I forgot. I'll work harder to . . ."

"That's what you always say!" His father interrupted. "How am I going to take you at your word if you fail me all the time? Well? How?"

Elliot knew that from this point on his explanation was unimportant. He would do or tell his father anything, anything at all, to turn away the scalding fury on his father's face. "I-I don't know, sir. I promise to do better. And I'll clean Harvey right away," he added softly.

"Yes, you will," his father growled. "And you'll do it now, and without any dinner after. How else am I going to make you obey me? How else am I going to make a man out of you? Well?"

"I don't know, sir," answered a weary Elliot. "I'm sorry."

"I'm done here," his father pronounced. He turned and pounded up the stairs and out of the cellar, banging the door shut behind him.

And that's how it was. Punishment from his father or mother meant an airtight prosecution, a heavy scolding, and the removal of something Elliot liked. By now he had learned to live in order to avoid punishment. He got up every morning before dawn because he didn't want to appear lazy. Even if he had done all of his chores so well the night before that he had nothing to do until noon, he knew that sleeping late would draw criticism. "Elliot," his mother would say, "I can't believe there's nothing you need to do." With her hand on her tightly set chin, and her forefinger tapping her cheek, she would say, "I think I'll start giving you some of my work, since you've got so much free time. Hmm . . . Let me think . . ." And she would. Although he didn't know it, fear had quietly become his primary relational skill. Elliot navigated life by it.

He turned his thoughts back to the trail home. It led him through some of his favorite places: the Jolly Brook, as he called it, which, because of the babbling and laughing sounds it made, wouldn't let him be sad; the giant and dark oak tree, that depending upon the light, offered strength or drew it away in the darkening shadows; and the cave of stars, where, while hiding once for fear of his father's temper, Elliot discovered a hole in the ceiling the size of a man's head through which he could see the stars. As he walked toward home, his mind happily wandered here and there as if with friends, and he was glad for it.

But, cresting a hill, he could just see a thin line of smoke above the trees that announced his mother's cooking. Soon, he would be able to make out the dimly lit windows, as day turned to dusk. And he would be home.

That's when fear returned.

Elliot felt it come upon him in the same way he imagined cold armor might feel to a knight preparing for battle. There was a moment of icy shock that seized his breath and made his heart race. Never before had he been so alert to its presence, because never before had it been so absent. His mind pictured the daily event of pulling on heavy, leather gloves before facing chicken wrath, and it occurred to him how alike this moment was—only more vital. This was inside and unseen, where toughening up to prevent pain was a matter of life and death.

"Why do I do this?" he questioned.

"To save yourself," filled his mind.

39

"That's right," he thought. "It's the only way to live." Barricades to injury were better than bandages after the hurt.

Elliot accepted the steely protection fear offered and made his way home and to his chores.

HISTORY

"Hello, son," his mother said as Elliot entered. "Did you get all of your chores done?" It was the most important question she asked. To Elliot, it seemed that his mother, Hannah, needed this moment to find out if everything was in order for her husbands' coming home from work. She scrutinized him because she was soon to be examined herself.

"Yes, mother," he answered.

"So you combed, curried and fed Harvey, mucked his stall, and put the chickens away, right? You got them all in?" she asked.

"I did," he replied.

His mother drew in a long breath, and let out an equally long sigh. "Good. Then everything's ready."

Elliot began moving toward the cellar door, where he could escape his mother's examination, but failed to reach its safety before she asked, "Did anything unusual happen today?" He froze at the top of the stairs, his mind racing to find a response. "Oh, no," he thought,

"How could she know?" In the delay, she said, "Because I thought I saw smoke . . . more than usual. Like a building was burning."

In the relief that felt like an instantaneous spring thaw, Elliot began to tell her about the fire that burned down the church.

"You didn't have anything to do with it, did you, Elliot?" she probed.

"No, mother. Of course not," he answered.

"As much as I don't like Reverend Fortner," she continued, "I wouldn't want the church to burn. And I really wouldn't want him to have anything against us that we'd have to hear about from now 'til eternity. So, just to be sure, you had nothing to do with it? Not you nor your friends?"

"No, ma'am," offered Elliot.

While it would have been bad enough had he played a part in the burning of the church, Hannah's primary concern was what it would do to their reputation. Had Elliot been responsible for the church fire, her greatest concern was not Elliot's guilt, but how to manage things. She was digging into Elliot for details, because her care was elsewhere. "I'm glad you weren't involved; there's a good boy."

Elliot was usually complimented by his mother more for what he didn't do than for what he did. "You're a Samuelson," she'd say, "and I don't want anyone getting a bad idea about us because of you." Trained by years of experience, Elliot was more afraid of doing something wrong than hopeful of doing something right. Home and reputation in town were the two stages upon which Hannah could set up and choreograph, so she worked tirelessly upon her actors. She was vigilant.

When talking about school, no matter how she formed her questions, she was actually probing about how Elliot had done socially. "How was class?" meant, "Did you have any ugly moments or fights or failures that I should be concerned about?" "How was lunch?" meant, "Tell me who you sat or played with, and if you said or did anything embarrassing." Even, "Do you have any school work you must do for tomorrow?" meant, "I don't want to have to face your teacher's criticism for work you failed to do." It wasn't that Hannah didn't care at all for Elliot—when Harvey threw him from the saddle one day, she was genuinely alarmed—it was just that she was so given to managing him for her greater concern that they seldom shared true warmth. They were a family, not for the value of being together and of supporting one another, but in order to accomplish something else, something notable and praiseworthy.

Elliot's mother wanted them to look like a perfect family, with nary a tarnished moment of image failure. Though she couldn't have told anyone exactly what the perfect family was, still she knew that she had to work diligently for fear of failing. Her husband didn't help—or wouldn't—and regularly violated her hopes by being too argumentative, too loose or too common in town, particularly at the leather shop. Hannah knew it was a necessary avenue of income for her family, but she wanted Frank to rule the town from an elevated image of superiority, even while making glue. To Hannah, respect came not from getting her hands dirty in the mess of people's ugliness, but from showing them how to not be messy.

Every raised voice and pounded fist in the leather shop was an image error that needed to be cleared away and tidied up. Even the scent of glue on Frank's clothes when he arrived home was the evidence of an earlier error that she now had to correct.

"Frank," she'd say, "you know what I think about glue on your clothing. Couldn't you have avoided it?" For Frank to respond, "No, I couldn't" was to invite her to show him how to work better and more efficiently in his shop—his area of expertise. That was too much to bear, so Elliot's father bowed to her prosecution and answered with a sullen, "Yes, I could have."

But it didn't end there because it didn't begin there.

Frank and Hannah Samuelson were together for many years before marriage and time had brought Elliot. In the same way as players on a team, they were together and worked at getting along so a desired goal could be accomplished. Their best moments were spent in strategy. Unified, they would discuss the many shortcomings and weaknesses of the people of Sarx, and how they might gain advantage. It was their game and their hope, focused for Frank at the leather shop and for Hannah as she postured nobility during gatherings large and small. In truth, they believed they were assisting lesser beings who, if and as they followed Samuelson leadership, would benefit in the long run—a run that never actually arrived anywhere but behind the Samuelsons.

Their worst moments were also spent in strategy—against each other. That they were opponents was not at once apparent, because it was veiled in the deceptive and nuanced dance of spousal management. Each had an ear upon their own inner rhythm so all that was needed were the proper steps and a willing partner. When life is about securing benefits, it doesn't stop with a wedding ring. Years of the dance meant moving the other without the burden of the other realizing—or resenting—who was in the lead. And, if you're going to dance, you'll need to look like you know what you're doing and that you enjoy it, even as you're preparing to introduce a different step to a different tune. While some might identify selfishness and arrogance as the motivators, they were only cousins to the true influence upon Frank and Hannah—fear. From a young age, each had found that life was good only if you controlled it.

Hannah despised the criticism and scorn she endured as a child. Her parents not only didn't care about what other people thought, but regularly gave them reasons to think poorly. Her father was an angry and loud-mouthed man, sometimes given to too much drink, which together produced the worst kind of family humiliation:

public. Hannah was known more for who her father was than for who she was. Her early life was overwhelmed by a much larger life.

When she was about 12 years old, she began to adopt the community's disdain for her father because it set her apart from him. If he were not going to change (and she couldn't change him), she would become one of them—and live better. As usual, her mother made no objection, which was her way of life. It wasn't that she didn't care, but that she believed everyone had to find his or her own way, no matter what anyone else thought . . . or what might help things go smoothly in a crowd. Her three older brothers were the most disrespectful and antagonistic people she knew, and grew up treating people decently only if it gave them what they wanted. It was their art form. They got what they wanted—there was that—but no one thought well of them. True to form, Hannah's mother believed it was *their way.* Hannah despised her for it.

She and Frank grew up around each other at school. For several years, it was *way around*, since neither liked the other. But opportunity for friendship came during a typical schoolyard argument one cold winter's day when the two found themselves taking the same side. Because their unity came by way of successfully ridiculing and embarrassing a mutual foe, Hannah and Frank instantly admired shared ability, and their way forward was formed.

Frank's navigational course was set on sarcasm—not the good-natured kind that brought smiles to everyone, but the kind that was the true meaning of the word: the tearing of flesh. Words of sarcasm are no less harmful a blow when one cannot see the wound. A verbal slash to the inside could be more damaging, with longer-lasting effects, than a wound on the outside. Because Frank wasn't much of a student, nor an athlete, well-crafted and well-placed sarcastic comments gave him a chance both to defend himself and to be noticed. No one else in his family of two older sisters and a younger brother had quite the same knack or use for it, so Frank was at the top of the sarcasm pyramid. He liked that.

Teaming up with Hannah created a formidable couple, and marriage at 18 was simply natural. Frank got a teammate, and Hannah got out.

10

TRUST

E lliot was curious about pigs, but their smell slapped at him. He anticipated the moment when the stench of mud and waste and pig would first assault his nose during morning chores, so he held his breath when nearing the pigpen to feed them. Well before they could see him, they would know he was coming, and begin squealing and jostling against each other for position. Though Elliot distributed the food in the trough as equitably as he could, still the pigs believed it was necessary to fight for advantage. "Crazy creatures" he thought.

"They really are something, aren't they?" Perfect said, suddenly standing just behind Elliot. Startled, Elliot dropped the feed bucket into the trough. "Let me get that for you," said Perfect, who climbed over the low fence of the pigpen.

"But, but," stammered Elliot, "it's awful in there and the pigs aren't to be trusted. And when did you get here?"

"Don't worry about me, my friend," said Perfect. "I know my way around pigs and mud," he chuckled, "and I'm not afraid to get dirty."

Because it was rare that anyone entered the pigpen, the pigs were immediately nervous, scattering and squealing their disapproval. "You are well, little ones," Perfect said, happily. "You are well, and needn't fear me." As if speaking their language, the pigs calmed instantly, and returned to the feeding trough to continue in all things pig.

"How did you do that?" asked Elliot, wonder filling his face.

His father was the only one to ever enter the pigpen, and then not without a rod and strong knife. "Pigs are dangerous, son," he would say. "They'll tear you up and eat you, given half a chance. You stay out of there, hear me?" Elliot didn't need to be told twice. Their long, sharp teeth sent the same message, particularly when they were nervous. Pigs were most frightening when they nervously opened and slammed shut their mouths, as if biting the air, saliva flying. But there was none of that now.

"Isn't it a fine morning, Elliot?" asked Perfect.

"Well, yes, it is," he replied. "But when did you get here? And where did you come from?"

"Those are good questions, Elliot," said Perfect, smiling. "Tell me, what do you think?"

Elliot looked around quickly. "I don't know. I don't see your horse."

"Oh, he's here," said Perfect, eyes wide and knowing. "He's just out of sight."

With a frown, Elliot asked, "So you let him wander around? You don't tether him?"

"Ha, ha," laughed Perfect. "No. There's no need. He's completely trustworthy, I assure you." He looked into Elliot's eyes. "I think the same of you, Elliot."

"But you don't know me. You might think otherwise if you did."

"But I do know you, Elliot, and I trust you with all of my heart. What do you think of that?"

"Well," replied Elliot, "I don't know how you know me, but my parents sure don't trust me. And they know me."

Looking around slowly, Perfect said, "Oh, I think they do, Elliot. They've left the care of all this to you, and they do it all the time. Even today."

It was true. Frank and Hannah often left him alone to care for the animals, but in a way that made him feel nervous . . . threatened. The fear of failure and punishment were constants to Elliot, no less so than on this day, when his parents could be gone for the whole day.

"It doesn't feel like they trust me," said Elliot. "It feels like they leave everything to me so they can go do what they want. If something bad happened around here, well, . . ." His voice sank and his eyes fell toward the muddy ground.

"I understand," said Perfect. "They do the best they can with what they know, Elliot. But I don't trust you that way. I trust you with my life."

Lifting his gaze from the ground to meet Perfect's eyes, Elliot asked, "But how can you? Who are you to trust me? And why would you trust me?"

"More good questions, my friend. Walk a bit with me, won't you?"

Together they walked from the barnyard in the direction of the well. As they did, Perfect said, "I am one who serves. I am one who gives life and who does not ask for it in return. I am one who loves. What do you think of that, Elliot?"

Before he could answer, they were met by the horse, which nuzzled up to Perfect. Elliot, making no effort to hide his wonder, said, "I—I don't know what to say. I'm not sure I know exactly what you mean, but I think I believe you. Why is that?"

The horse nodded its head into Perfect, moving him momentarily off balance. Perfect laughed and took the horse's head into his hands. "Yes. You know, don't you?" He swung up into the saddle and grinned. "Until tomorrow, Elliot, when we'll talk about that."

"You have to go?" asked Elliot. "But there's so much I want to ask you, so much I don't know."

Looking kindly upon him, Perfect said, "You will enjoy the truth, Elliot. You were made for the truth."

Without so much as a touch or a word to the horse, the two began moving toward the trees surrounding the Samuelson's. "One more thing," said Perfect over his shoulder. "With me you will have everything." Before Elliot could respond, Perfect vanished into the light.

With a sense of happy bafflement, Elliot turned toward the barn-yard and muttered, "I was hoping he'd feed the chickens." It was the happiest moment he'd had in a long time.

11

ATTENTION

A nd that's how it was for Elliot and Perfect, who met him each day in an unexpected moment. Really, it became a secret joke for the two of them. Elliot could tell that Perfect got as much pleasure out of showing up in a surprising moment as he did. It might be on the way to school or somewhere in the barnyard or on an errand for his mother; he never knew when or where.

Although Elliot at first fretted about what their sudden meetings might require of him or how he might have to explain to his parents what was happening, never did Perfect appear in a way that forced anything from him. Their secret meetings became the anticipated gift and certainty of every day. Almost by accident, Elliot changed.

"Why are you smiling, Pig Boy?" demanded Nancy Eaton, who threw the question at Elliot on the playground in the same way one might throw a rock. Interrogation was her way of communicating with Elliot because she might find something useful for the proof of her superiority. While she was, in fact, curious, and noticed a change about Elliot, she felt insulted that anyone so miserable as he could be inexplicably happy. She felt wronged.

"Oh, I don't know," answered a suddenly cautious Elliot. "No reason, I guess." He knew better than to give Nancy anything more than a general response, having been examined and found painfully faulty many times before.

"Well, you sure look goofy with that stupid smile on your face, Samuelson," she sneered. "And where's that three dollars you owe me for the mess you made of my jacket? Did you think I forgot about that? Do I have to tell my brothers?" she threatened.

While Elliot hadn't forgotten, three dollars was an impossible amount for him to get. He'd agreed to the penalty only to escape the immediate pressure of the event—fear of the Eaton brothers. "I'm, ah, working on it, Nancy," Elliot said, the smile now gone. He had no better answer.

Naturally, Nancy was not impressed. "Do you think I don't see what you're doing, Samuelson? I'll give you until next Monday to give it to me, or I'll tell my brothers. Understand?" To Nancy, "*understand*" never meant, "do you comprehend," but "do you know what peril awaits if you fail?"

Elliot had no way out that he could think of, so he replied, "Yes, Nancy. I'll try."

As Nancy marched away, Elliot lamented aloud, "I wish Perfect was here."

"What if I am?" came the immediate reply. Whirling around, Elliot searched for his friend, but could not find him.

"Where are you? I know your voice, yet I don't see you," said Elliot.

"But you know I'm here. Is that okay, Elliot?" asked Perfect.

"Well, I suppose so. But I'm not sure," replied Elliot. "I mean I can't be seen talking to no one, can I? People would think I'm crazy."

"Good point, Elliot," laughed Perfect. "I'll meet you later and we'll talk about it."

As Elliot and his classmates jostled back into school after lunch and were seated, it occurred to Elliot that his meetings with Perfect had become more important to him than anything else. It wasn't that Nancy Eaton or Miss Breckett or fear of failing his parents didn't still cause him concern, it was that he was so fascinated with Perfect—and so happy in the fascination—that everything else, everything that had been so big and heavy and foreboding, had grown smaller and lighter.

Thinking upon it, he was unaware of Miss Breckett's question, cheerfully pointed at him with deadly accuracy. "Well, Elliot?" she asked. "Alright, would someone please wake Mr. Samuelson so we can all learn what's occupying his mind more than his class work?" Miss Breckett stretched out the word "more" so that it nearly had a tune all to itself.

Dan Westerly poked his elbow into Elliot's ribs, which immediately brought him to full alert.

"Um, what, Miss Breckett?"

With a loud burst, every face in the classroom erupted into laughter. After a punishing delay, Miss Breckett waved the class to quiet and said with a brilliant smile, "It would seem, Mr. Samuelson, that you have better things to do than to pay attention."

"Actually, Miss Breckett, I *was* paying attention, but not to you," answered Elliot, "and I apologize."

A cold and eerie hush emptied the room of laughter, replaced by gasps of shock. Lowering her head, Miss Breckett fixed her eyes upon Elliot in a way that no one had ever seen. The constant smile vanished, replaced by drawn lips, a tightly clenched jaw, and cold, unblinking eyes. It was so quiet that everyone could hear her take a deep breath and release it slowly, measuring her response. Suddenly an audience to an epic battle, everyone else held their breath.

"I'm sorry, Miss Breckett," repeated Elliot. "I'll try to do better now." And, for the slightest moment, Miss Breckett's face softened. It was almost kindly. Not everyone saw it, but Elliot did.

With an abrupt jerk and a gasp of air, she regained her composure, re-animated her smile, and turning warmly to the rest of the students, said, "See that you do, Mr. Samuelson. Everyone will appreciate it, won't we class?" With oxygen again filling their lungs, everyone voiced their relieved approval. Elliot, on the other hand, could scarcely manage another word, because the trauma of the moment was only just beginning to recede.

He hadn't meant to be rude to Miss Breckett. Elliot had simply given no consideration to his response to her question other than the truth. His friendship with Perfect had begun to shape his involvement with others, but he hadn't known how much until he failed to frame himself properly in Miss Breckett's classroom. She was so skilled in shaping how people managed themselves that no one actually considered how imprisoning it was. At least, children didn't. Adults, however, avoided her like shadows the sunlight. Her sunny disposition demanded an equally sunny reflection, and while most people managed a returned smile in her presence, they fled as quickly as possible.

Elliot considered what had just happened. How could he have been so careless? He knew better than to cross Miss Breckett. Still, she hadn't truly punished him, although there was plenty of time left in the school day for that. And why, after his fairly blurted apology, had her face become almost kindly? It was all a little frightening and out of control to him, so he gave his mind back to arithmetic and to Miss Breckett's restored sunshine.

12

ALWAYS

"What were you thinking, Samuelson?" asked Don Nibecker. Everyone was pushing their way out of the school, and for a short time, Elliot could not avoid Don.

"About what?" Elliot replied.

"Oh, come on. You know! In class!"

Elliot paused and thought for a moment. "Well, I don't know. I was thinking about something else and I, um, I didn't care about what I said. That's it."

"In Miss Breckett's class, you always have to be careful, you idiot," said Don. "Everybody knows. I can't believe you were so stupid."

Elliot sighed. "I know. You're right. I was just distracted. I forgot myself."

"Well, it was sure crazy, I'll say that. We all thought Miss Breckett was going to kill you or something. As much as I think you're an idiot, I don't want you dead." It was the least abrasive thing that Don had ever said to Elliot.

"Um, thanks," Elliot answered. See you tomorrow."

"Yeah, sure." The two parted, heading in opposite directions.

But before Elliot could escape to the safety of the woods on his way home, Donna Jensen grabbed his shoulder and asked, "What got into you, Samuelson? What's the matter with you?"

Turning to face her, Elliot fumbled for a response. While Donna wasn't as mean as Nancy Eaton, the two were allies as far as Elliot was concerned. Anything he said would surely be relayed to Nancy. "Well, I—I don't know," he answered. "What's the big deal?"

When around people he feared, one of Elliot's maneuvers was not actually answering a question that could get him into trouble. He'd learned that people often didn't really want an answer to a question, but an angle on how to more effectively put him down.

"*What's the big deal?*" Donna sneered. "The big deal is that no one ever crosses Miss Breckett—she's too nice! We had no idea what was going to happen next. Couldn't you feel that, Samuelson?"

Elliot's response didn't help. "You mean when I said I was sorry?" Donna's eyes flew open while her head cocked and her mouth readied to launch her response. But before she could, Elliot blurted, "*Ohh!* You mean when I said I hadn't been paying attention to her. You mean that, right?"

"Yes, of course I mean that!"

"I don't know. I guess I just wasn't worried about what to say."

"How could you not be?" demanded Donna. "Aren't you always worried? I am." Realizing that she had admitted more than felt safe, Donna quickly filtered herself. "I mean, *sometimes* I worry. You know, like when I might get into trouble for saying something I shouldn't. Why weren't you afraid like that?"

Because he didn't really know, Elliot answered, "I just forgot, okay? I was thinking about something else and I forgot to worry. I—I'll be more careful."

"Well, I should think so. I've never felt so much, so much . . ." Struggling for the right words, Donna continued, "so much fear at what might happen. Why is that? Miss Breckett wouldn't hurt anyone, would she?"

Elliot shrugged. "I don't guess so. But I'm sure afraid of her. At least before now, I was."

"Well, I think fear is a good thing!" Donna remarked. "I mean, what would we do without it? It keeps me out of a lot of trouble, I don't mind saying. Maybe you need some more, Samuelson. One more crazy thing like that and I don't know what will happen!"

Elliot was ready to head home. "Well, I don't know, but I'll pay better attention from now on . . . or at least not say something as dumb as that."

Donna smiled. "Good idea, Elliot, good idea."

With that, the two parted and Elliot turned to the way home. Rounding the last corner before entering the woods, he was deep in thought. Elliot had for many years been entirely self-centered, although not in a way that anyone would have easily recognized. Actually, he did his level best to do what people wanted so he could avoid trouble. Fear owned his relationships. With conflict and trouble ever near, being alert at all times was a skill required for life. "Self-centered" meant "self-preservation," so it made no sense that he would have forgotten himself in the classroom, one of the most dangerous places he knew. To Elliot, going to school was more about the pain of learning he had disappointed others than about learning how to learn. Indeed, Elliot would not have gone to school if his parents had not forced him. "You've got to make something of yourself," they said. He assumed they were right, but he still didn't like it. Elliot thought it all felt only a little different from how he trained the animals at home, except that Miss Breckett was the trainer at school.

"What if I go with you?" asked Perfect.

Elliot looked quickly around because he was again unaware that Perfect was near. Glad and relieved, Elliot asked, "Where are you?"

"Oh, just out of sight," replied Perfect. "But I'm with you. I am always with you, Elliot."

Elliot pondered what that meant. "That explains a lot . . . and that means a lot. You're always with me? *Always*?"

"Always," said Perfect. "I will never leave you alone, Elliot."

"Well, then you might know what happened in Miss Breckett's class. I was scared. I've never felt anything like that."

"Actually, I think you've felt that many times before," said Perfect, "but have grown accustomed to it . . . until now that is."

"What do you mean?" asked Elliot.

"You felt the power of fear, Elliot, and how people use it as an advantage to get what they want. You've grown up with it. As one uses a tool, so fear is commonly used, but you don't feel that from me."

Eyes focused and wide open, Elliot spoke carefully. "I think I understand. You told me that you serve, give, and love and don't require anything from me. I've never known anyone like you, who didn't make me feel like I had to be anything different, or like I didn't have to be careful around them. I think I might've always been scared around people, except with you. I was thinking about you when Miss Breckett called my name, and that's when I got afraid. She makes me afraid."

"There are people who use fear," replied Perfect, "and there are people who are used by fear, Elliot. Which one are you? You're learning what life is like with me, in contrast to what life has been. What do you think?"

"I don't know," Elliot answered, "but everything is so different with you. Actually, you scare me too, but not like Miss Breckett. It's like you interrupt me and what I'm doing all the time, and I'm afraid at first. But it never lasts because of how you are with me."

Perfect laughed. "Well, that's good."

Elliot concluded, "I think that I am more *used by fear* than I am a *user of fear*. Is that right, Perfect?"

"It is, but why do you think so?"

"I'm not sure. It's just that when you're with me, I'm not afraid. But as soon as others get around me, I feel like I have to be careful because I might get into trouble or do something stupid. Is that fear using me?"

"It is," said Perfect, "but you have noticed that with me, fear loses its power. I neither use fear nor am I used by it; fear has no place with me, Elliot. Why do you think that is?"

Elliot grew pensive for a moment. "I think you actually like me and aren't trying to change me. It's like you bring out the best of me, or like I am better because of you. Is that right?"

In the light quickly drawn together, Perfect appeared before Elliot.

"I am happy you think so," said Perfect, "and yes; you are better with me. Isn't that good to know, Elliot?" Tears filled Perfect's eyes. "You once asked who I am and what I do. Do you remember that, Elliot?"

"Yes, I do."

"Have you come to any answers?"

Elliot thought carefully. "It seems to me that everywhere I go, everything I need to know, and the hope that I have—it's all with you." The truth of what Elliot knew surprised him, and with unrestrained joy, he burst out, "Perfect, *I love you!*"

"Yes, you do!" said Perfect, as he drew near and embraced Elliot. "Has anything else become clear to you?"

"I think so," answered Elliot. "I think I love you because you love me. Is that right, Perfect? Do you love me?"

"*I do!*" cried Perfect, still holding onto him. "I do love you! It's what I do best. Elliot, you know who I am and what I do. You have described me just right."

"Perfect, I know that I never want to be apart from you."

Perfect hugged him tighter. "And you never have to be. Never ever. Not for one moment. You have seen me appear many times before you, haven't you, Elliot?"

Elliot nodded.

"Just as you have seen me appear before you, so it is that I can be *within* you for always and for everything. You would be as close to me as you could possibly be. Would you like that, Elliot?"

Drawing back his head from Perfect's chest, Elliot asked, "You can? You can do that? You *would* do that?"

Perfect smiled warmly, "Yes, Elliot. You would be my happiest place to be."

Joy lit Elliot's face. "Then yes! There is nothing I want more than you. And I know why you have that name, Perfect. You are Perfect with me."

"*I am!*" exclaimed Perfect, laughing heartily.

In a breath of a moment, Perfect was at once lit up, only to vanish. Elliot gasped, his eyes wide open. A parade of fearful thoughts that once controlled him raced across his mind and vanished. In their place was love.

13

INSIDE

A smile the size of the barn stretched across Elliot's face. He couldn't contain it, and didn't even think he should. "Perfect?" he asked, placing his hands upon his chest. "Are you here? Oh, I know you must be because, . . . I, I don't know how to say it, but the way you are *with me* now feels the way you are *in me*. Is that right, Perfect? Are you here?"

"I am, Elliot. I am here," replied Perfect.

Tears suddenly flowed down Elliot's cheeks. "I'm so glad, Perfect! And I think hearing you is just like it was when you talked with me without appearing to me. Is that right?"

"I love you, Elliot," replied Perfect.

"I can hear you!" Elliot shouted with joy. "I can! Only it's different. There's more. So much more now."

Perfect asked, "Why do think that is, Elliot?"

With wonder lighting his face, Elliot replied, "Is it because you're in me now, instead of just nearby?"

"Yes, that is why. What else do you know? What else do you feel, Elliot?"

"I'm not sure, exactly, but I feel, um, *safe*, which is new for me. And what happened to my worries? What happened to fear?"

"As you have known before with me," replied Perfect, "so you now know more completely. Where I am known, fear is not welcome, because who I am and what I do drive it out. There is so much that is new, Elliot! I will show you when you get home."

Elliot hadn't thought of going home, but considering it now produced an odd feeling. Before he could think any further, he blurted out, "I don't want to go home! Perfect, what will happen there? Now that you're in me, what will become of me? What must I do? Oh, I'm afraid . . ."

"Elliot, I am not asking you to do anything at all," interrupted Perfect. "You have noticed that fear has just now spoken to you, and while you have long agreed to live by fear's direction, your agreement is at an end. I am here with you, and you do not get along with fear anymore—you can feel that. Fear is not welcome anymore because you have me, and we will go everywhere together. Do you believe me, Elliot?"

"I do believe you, Perfect, but thinking about being at home with my father and mother and you is, well, I don't know what will happen. I don't know what I will do. It feels dangerous."

"Yes, it is!" exclaimed Perfect. "But only because fear has kept you hiding at home. Fear has promised to lead you away from harm, but it punishes you for following. Fear has meant a caged life for you, Elliot—like one of your chickens—but I will bring you out, and you will know how I am with you. I will be with you, and will never harm you. Do you believe me, Elliot?"

"You have never been wrong," Elliot replied.

The two of them began walking through the woods toward home, although anyone watching would have seen only Elliot striding through the thick stands of pine and aspen. Elliot was Perfect's home, so no matter where he went, there was Perfect—at home.

"As happy as you are for me to be in you, Elliot, I am even more. It is my highest joy to be always in you, for there is nothing we will not do together. Although the days to come will be different from any you have known, I will see to it that you know me—how I am with you, and how I am with others. What do you think of that?"

"I guess I'm both hopeful and anxious," Elliot replied aloud. He laughed and asked. "Now that you're inside, should I speak out loud or just think thoughts toward you?"

Perfect laughed, too. "Yes! The answer is 'yes,' Elliot. Any way you choose will please me, because I delight in being involved with you."

"Perfect, will it take long for me to get used to you being in me?" asked Elliot.

"That is a good question, my friend. You have been accustomed to living without me, and have learned the lie that life must be what happens around you. This requires skills to get what you want and don't want, of course, which has made you a lonely slave to what happens in your days. With me inside, this has all changed. I have interrupted and ended that slavery by giving you real life from me. Do you understand this, Elliot?"

"Hmm." Elliot cocked his head and laughed again. "Just how involved are you going to be, Perfect?"

"As much as you want," Perfect replied. "Perhaps a little more, actually, but you won't mind. You'll see. I really am Perfect."

Elliot felt flooded with joy. "I think I'm understanding that more and more."

"As you have thoughts and feelings," said Perfect, "so do I. Sometimes I will tell you my thoughts, just as I am now. Other times you will feel what I am feeling. You will like that, but it can be confusing, since thoughts and feelings that are not mine have been present with you all of your days. Mine are very different from those, and you will enjoy mine."

"But won't I get confused?" asked Elliot.

"Yes, sometimes you will," Perfect answered, "but together we will make that happen less and less. I will see to it—do not worry. This will be wonderful, Elliot, and you will enjoy life with me."

14

LOVE

Standing at the door, Elliot drew a deep breath and stepped inside. His mother was not immediately visible, so because there were chores to be done, he walked down the stairs to the cellar and changed from school clothes into work ones. Since he did most of his chores alone outside, Elliot felt a freedom outside the house that he did not inside. He quickly went back up the stairs, glanced briefly about the kitchen, and made his exit.

"Oh, come on!" he heard his mother say.

Turning toward the barn, Elliot saw his mother bending over in the garden, hair pulled back, wrestling with something in the ground. Her gloved hands were seized around what could only be an old tree root, and she struggled with all of her considerable might to rip it from the earth.

"Come out of there!" she commanded. "I hate you!"

Elliot didn't like to work with his mother in the garden because it was the one place where she was reckless. The return of a weed, an appearance of a pest, or something that wasn't growing and producing as it should, set her off, making her become the crazy mother he feared. She seemed dangerous.

But just then, watching her angrily pull and yank on the unyielding root, a different image filled his mind, one that he'd never known. Elliot suddenly didn't think of Hannah, his mother, the woman he'd always known. Instead, he thought of Hannah, a woman he'd never really known, with a history secret to herself. He saw her, without any of the shared experiences that would make him respond to her, even to avoid her. "What is this?" he wondered. Elliot was drawn to his mother. With tears in his eyes, he cared and longed for her more than he feared her, a reversal of what he had felt before around her. What filled him now was the desire to hug his mother—dangerous, dirty, frazzled Hannah—a woman alone in life.

"But what will happen?" he worried. "What will she do?"

"You don't know," replied Perfect, "but you love her. And that's me with you, Elliot."

"I do love her, and I really like that!" thought Elliot, "but I'm terrified. If I go to her, she might be angry with me, and I wouldn't know what to do then. Oh, Perfect, it would hurt so much!"

"Yes, it would," said Perfect. "But the love you now know, especially for your mother, is better and more powerful than any hurt she might cause. I am with you, Elliot, and nothing can separate you from my love—even now with your mother. No matter what."

Moved by love, Elliot took a few short steps toward the garden. As he walked, he became aware of something odd at the edge of his thinking. Fear was at a distance, noisily clamoring for his attention, and warning him of what might happen—*doom*. Yet love flowed and moved all the greater toward his mother.

"Yes, Elliot," said Perfect, "fear wants your attention, but you are no longer friends, and you see it as the cowering thief it is. Follow love."

And he did.

When he was twenty feet from his mother, Hannah released the root, straightened up and unknowingly turned toward her oncoming son. "Elliot," she said, wiping sweat from her forehead, "I didn't know you were home, but I'm glad you are because . . ." Before she could finish, Elliot embraced her with everything in him. In that moment, love was consummated—it came together in and through Elliot. There was no place he would have rather been than in love expressed to his mother.

"Well, well, Elliot. What's all this?" Hannah asked. Although she accepted the hug with all of the affection of a pine tree, Elliot held on. In love that knew no fault with his mother, he was free to enjoy the full effect.

"I just want you to know that I love you, mother," he said, face pressed into her chest. Hannah fidgeted a bit, uncomfortable with the unusual. But then her arms and hands moved ever so slowly, up and out and around Elliot, there to rest. She didn't fully return his hug, but it didn't matter to Elliot. Love was more important.

"Thank you, son," Hannah said, with just a hint of emotion.

There was nothing more for Elliot to say—he had said it, and that was all he knew in the moment. Several satisfying seconds later, he loosened his hug, and asked, "How may I help you, mother?"

Flustered, but collecting herself, she answered, "Well, I don't know. I was going to say, um, ah, that you could, ah . . ."

"Help you with that old tree root?" Elliot offered.

"Yes," said Hannah. "That's exactly it. Darn thing seemed to show up here overnight, I swear, and I can't budge it."

"What if we both grab hold of it?" he suggested. "Maybe we can get it out together."

Like surgeons examining a patient, Elliot and Hannah surveyed the root, agreed upon angles and hand placements, and began to pull. The reluctant root moved just a little, and small fissures began to appear in the soil as they worked.

"We can do this," grunted Elliot.

"I think we can!" gasped Hannah. "Let's give it everything we've got! Pull, son, pull!"

With a cracking sound, the earth released its captive and the root came free. Like winning a game of tug-of-war, Elliot and Hannah crashed together to the ground in a heap of root and flying dirt.

"We did it!" yelled Hannah. "We did it!"

Wiping dirt from his face and clothes, Elliot laughed. "You're a dirty mess, mother! You should see yourself!"

Hannah laughed, too. "Look who's talking, son! But who cares? We did it, and it was worth it."

Sitting together in the dirt and grime of their effort, mother and son smiled at each other.

15

JOY

"Woo-hooooo!" said Elliot, as he lifted a shovel hanging from the barn wall. "That was wonderful!" he thought, delighted by what had happened with his mother. Tears in his eyes didn't really bother him as he began to shovel Harvey's stall because he was so happy. "My goodness, you've been busy, haven't you?" he asked, scooping and moving the mess into the wheelbarrow. Harvey was silent.

Navigating the wheelbarrow past his father's workbench and out of the barn, Elliot was barely aware of the increasingly foul smell as he drew alongside the pigpen. "Well, 'hello' to you, too," he chuckled as the pigs, alarmed by his presence, produced their usual chorus of snorts. Elliot reasoned with them. "Oh, come on now. It's just me, your friend, Elliot. "

As he tilted the wheelbarrow forward, its contents sliding and fumbling onto the manure pile, Elliot cried out, "Oh, Perfect! I'm so, so . . . Oh, I don't know what I am! All I know is that I've never been so happy, so glad as I am right now. What is this I'm feeling?" In the silence of no reply, Elliot thought through what had just occurred.

"I have never loved my mother like that—not ever," he thought, "and it felt so good. And I've never seen her like that . . . like, like, she wasn't only my mother, but somehow I knew her differently . . . *better*. And I wanted to hug her, without anybody telling me to. But it wasn't all easy. There was fear of what might happen. But you told me to follow love, and not fear, so I did. And, oh, my mother! I could've hugged her for hours. Perfect, it felt like all of the hugs I could have hugged her with for a long time came together in that one hug. Is that right?"

"Yes, Elliot," replied Perfect, "and you felt my hug hugging her, too. Together we loved Hannah, and you saw that she felt truly loved, didn't you?"

"Yes, I think she did. Maybe she didn't do it very well, but I sure did. Well, you and I did. Should we keep hugging her?"

"As much as you want, Elliot," replied Perfect.

Elliot laughed. "I might want to all the time. This is going to be all new, isn't it, Perfect? If it means more of this, well, I'm already crazy happy with joy. But why didn't you talk with me when I was in the barn? Don't you like the barn?"

Perfect chuckled in return. "You were enjoying yourself so much that I wanted you to think about what had happened without me saying anything about it. You are learning so much about life with me, Elliot, and it is good for you to explore all of this."

"Why did fear try to stop me?" asked Elliot.

"That is a good question. Fear is one of many thoughts and feelings that will try to get you to do something without me, which is no way for you to live now, since you and I are together. Do you understand this, Elliot?"

"Yes, I think so. As I began to walk toward my mother to hug her with you, fear told me a reason to stop. I am so glad I didn't, because I would have missed her! I think I've been missing my mother for a long time. Is that fear's fault, Perfect?"

"Without me, you've had little choice but to follow the way of fear, even while making it appear okay."

"Oh, but now I know it's not okay!" cried Elliot. "I don't ever want to miss this, this joy with you that fear would steal."

"I am very happy to hear that, Elliot, because it is very important. For that reason I wanted you to think about what you thought and felt and did with me. Because we are together now, you are safe and secure and have everything you will ever need. So it's important for you to recognize anything that makes you think otherwise. Fear is a liar; its only language insists that you have to accomplish something by yourself because being together with me is not enough. As I have told you, you and I are not friends with fear, so you must be aware of its language."

"Will fear bother me always?" asked Elliot.

"Well, 'yes' and 'no'," Perfect replied. "You can tell that fear is not from you. It felt confusing and ugly on the way to love your mother, the very thing you most wanted to do. Fear is rude—it seeks to control you—and will be part of your experience, Elliot. But I will help you to see it and to use it as a way to deepen your trust in me. And you will like that."

"Oh, good," Elliot said, "because I sure love you and what we're doing together. And I am glad to know that fear is not from me, and that I don't have to follow it. Perfect, this joy I have with you is better than anything I have ever had."

"Yes, you and I do well together, don't we, Elliot? And this will help you to know and trust me and the ways I am when fear suggests a different course, a different way to live. There are many ways for you to know and be confident about me, Elliot, one of which is by talking with me. So when you do not hear me, as you didn't in the barn, look for other ways that I will be evidently with you. Always look for me, for I am always with you. I love you."

16

PEACE

"Elliot? Are you awake?" His father's loud voice could be heard through the cellar ceiling

"Yes, father."

"Good. Then come up here." Elliot hadn't heard his father come home the previous night, which was unusual. He didn't know if that was because his father had been unusually quiet, or because Elliot had been so happy that sleep came easily and quickly. No matter what, he knew better than to delay.

"I'm in trouble," he thought. He rapidly searched through the memory of yesterday's chores to see if he had forgotten something, anxiously sifting each task for error. As he hurriedly dressed, a familiar sense of dread crept into his mind. "This is not going to be good," he thought, and began making his way up the cellar stairs.

And then he had another thought: "What about Perfect?" Jarred out of a half-sleep by his father, Elliot hadn't paused to think about all that had happened the day before. Oddly, it was gone from his mind—at least until that question. And then he asked another one. "What should I do about my father, Perfect?"

A single word came in answer: "Nothing."

"*Nothing*?" asked Elliot. And that's all there was.

But not entirely. A calm wave of peace moved within Elliot, all but vanquishing the anxiety that had seized him. He became more aware of the unusual peace within than he was concerned by the usual expression upon his father's face.

In the kitchen hunched over a cup of coffee, Frank Samuelson was the picture of a perpetually disappointed man. Indeed, when Elliot and his classmates had been given the assignment of making a drawing of their families, his caricature of his father caught Miss Breckett's attention.

"Why, Elliot! Surely your father is not so grumpy as this, is he? Perhaps you could cheer him up a little. If you were to use some brighter color and turn up his mouth, he would be oh-so-much happier." And then Miss Breckett said the words that forced him to comply: "Besides, what will Mr. Samuelson say when he sees what you've done? I'm certain you'll want him to like your work when you take it home. Isn't that right?"

While Elliot didn't believe that his father ever really *liked* his work, he was bothered by his faultfinding, and so altered his drawing. Miss Breckett was pleased, and his father's displeasure avoided.

Standing before his father now, Elliot felt caught between two forces: a dominant peace and a lesser anxiety. As far back as he could remember he had not known peace when commanded to appear before his father, so this was new.

"Elliot," his father said, "mother told me of the root she found in the garden. Did I not ask you to clear the soil last month?"

"Yes, sir," he replied. Although anxiety pressed at him, whispering instructions to harden himself against his father as a way of surviving the moment, Elliot instead thought of Perfect's promise to be with him at all times. Peace guarded and kept him free from following anxiety's defensive suggestions.

"How could you have missed it, son?"

"I wondered the same thing, father," answered Elliot, calmly. "As you asked, I cleared that area and cannot explain how I could have missed it . . . but I did." Strangely, Elliot's gaze was actually drawn to his father's eyes, not forced there as always before. And still, peace reigned.

"Yet, you and mother got it out after all, so there's that," his father said. "And she seemed to have enjoyed the whole filthy mess, though I cannot imagine why."

"Well, it *was* rather funny, father," Elliot replied. "Mother and I looked like Harvey after he has rolled in the corral."

Frank nodded. "I thought as much last night after seeing mother's clothing left in the mudroom. When I asked about it, she laughed and said it was the most fun she'd had in a long time. I just thought it was ridiculous and that it could have been avoided. But I couldn't argue with the result. Elliot, thank you for making mother laugh."

"We did laugh, father," said Elliot. "I think we were the dirtiest and ugliest we've ever been, but because we got the root out together, it made it fun."

"Well, please don't make a habit of not finishing your chores, son, and of needing mother to help. I wouldn't want mother falling into the manure pile because you didn't finish *that* chore!"

And that was it. Except that, free of anxiety, and before his father could leave the kitchen, Elliot grabbed him about the waist and hugged him tightly. And, for once, Frank hugged him back. "Why don't you come by the shop this afternoon, son, and I'll show you something I've been working on."

"Yes, father—after I get my chores done," Elliot replied with a smile.

Frank laughed. "That's right. First things first. See you later."

When he got outside, Elliot walked to the barn to begin his chores. "Perfect," he thought, "what just happened?"

"What do you mean, my friend?" Perfect replied.

"Well, I am almost always, um, nervous or something around my father, and always get myself as prepared as I can be to have a proper response. I don't relax until I'm away from him, fearful that something I've said or not said might make him mad or disappointed with me. I don't think I've ever realized how scared I am until just now."

"Why now?" asked Perfect. "What made the difference?"

"I knew you were with me. And even though you said for me to do nothing about my father, wasn't it you who made me feel more peace than fear?"

"Yes, Elliot, it was."

"That was amazing, Perfect. I don't think I would have noticed if I hadn't done as you said—*nothing*. Oh, Perfect, I'm so happy you're here with me, in me, because you make all the difference."

"Yes, I do," said Perfect. "We're good together, and you will see how I am with you, even though fear will tell you to do as you used to do, when we weren't together. You are new, Elliot."

Cleaning off his father's work table with a broom and barn rag, Elliot asked, "Will I always have peace like that, Perfect?"

"Something you will want to remember," Perfect answered, "is that *I am peace*, and you will always have me. You have not known peace. You have done things to avoid hardship or punishment, and at times that has momentarily worked out, but that is not the peace that I am. For that kind of peace you must work and earn, but it is always subject to loss. Fear lives there. The peace that I am you have not earned and can never lose, no matter what fear may tell you."

"I am so glad, because I could feel fear again," Elliot said, "like I was in the middle—between you two. Does that make sense?"

"Yes, it does," replied Perfect. "Fear wants to make friends with you and to influence you, but as you have discovered, it is no friend. It would make you hide, while I make you free. Did you realize that, Elliot?"

"I did!" said Elliot. "I did. Oh, I don't like fear, Perfect; I like you!"

Perfect chuckled. "Yes, you do. And I like you, Elliot. I am so glad that you felt the struggle—like a tug of war—between fear and me. It is our struggle, and not yours. But you remembered me, and I kept you secure in peace, and fear lost."

"I like peace, Perfect. And I'm glad that I don't have to do anything to get it as I have thought. I know I couldn't, anyway—I never have! Perfect, I love you. Thank you for showing me this morning that you are peace, and I have you."

"I am," said Perfect, "and I love you, Elliot."

17

PATIENCE

As Elliot rounded the corner of Ferrin's blacksmith barn and the school building came into view, Perfect said, "Today is our first day of school, Elliot. What do you think we will do together?"

"Well," said Elliot, "I don't know, except that you will be with me."

"Yes, I will," replied Perfect. "Let me ask you this; what do you think fear will try to do with you?"

Elliot paused and leaned against a fence. "I feel fear right now, Perfect. I'm going to see people I don't much like, and I'm already thinking of how to avoid them or keep them from, I don't know, bothering me."

"Do you think you will be successful?" asked Perfect.

"Probably not. No, I won't."

"Then you are ready for me," said Perfect. "Am I good with you, Elliot?"

"Oh, yes. You really are perfect with me."

"It's true, and nothing makes me happier than to be with you. So here's what I'd like you to do. Think of going to school with me today—where you are not bringing me to your school, but I am bringing you to mine."

With a look of surprise upon his face, Elliot replied, "But I know everyone here; you don't know anyone. I know how they all are and what they're going to do, and can prepare for it. Miss Breckett is going to be, well, you know, too happy, and . . . well, *scary*. Don Nibecker is going to be mean to me, and maybe steal my lunch, and then Nancy Eaton..."

"Yes, Elliot," Perfect interrupted, "Nancy will demand three dollars from you, I know. And she has already told her brothers, Tad and Tom, but they're not going to tear your arms off—don't worry,"

"*You know*?" asked Elliot. "How do you know all that?"

In a momentary pause, Elliot suddenly felt as though a cold, dark and long-present storm had blown out of his mind. In its place was a growing awareness, a new and vast understanding that made his eyes and mouth open wide in wonder. "So, so, you're everywhere? You know everything?"

"It would seem so, Elliot," Perfect happily replied.

"So, then what are you doing with them?" asked an incredulous Elliot.

"That is my life with them. This is my life with you."

"Do any of them know you like I know you, Perfect?"

"No. Not yet," Perfect replied. "Until now, everyone in Sarx has labored under the terrible tyranny of fear. It is all they have known. But, as you know, my time has come. And I am beginning with you, Elliot. What do you think about that?"

"Why me?"

"Why not you, Elliot?"

"I, I don't think I can answer that, Perfect. I don't know, but I'm sure glad you're with me. You must have plans for them, don't you?"

"Why, yes. I do," Perfect answered. "This is why you are at school with me today. Do you understand what I am saying, Elliot?"

"I think I do. You've been so good with me that I think you're going to affect people with me. Is that right, Perfect? Are you going to do something with me like what you did with my mother and father?"

"Aha! Now you've got it, although I won't have you hug everyone." Perfect laughed. "You and I are perfect together—we love and trust each other—and your mother and father have been affected by us. Have you enjoyed that, Elliot?"

"Yes!" exclaimed Elliot. "It has been exciting and mysterious, and a little scary, but these have been the best days I have ever had."

"Mine too," said Perfect. "My joy is full. Now, since you and I are together inside, I want you to be open to what I might want to do toward the outside. As we get to school, people will do something that gets your attention, and you will be inclined to respond in the manner that you always have. Elliot, may I interrupt that habit?"

Elliot pondered Perfect's question. "Hmm. Yes. Yes, you may. In fact, would you please, Perfect? You have to be better than I have been—I know you are! But I've got some trouble going on, just so you know."

"I do know," said Perfect, "and because fear has long motivated you to do something clever, defensive or aggressive that seemed to offer a good way through each situation, think of me as often as you like today, at any moment, during any situation, good or bad. By thinking of me, you will interrupt fear's usual influence upon you, and I will be evident. You will like that."

As Elliot approached the schoolhouse, the bell began to ring, urging him forward. He quickened his pace, easily imagining Sally laboring with the bell rope. Aloud, Elliot mocked, "Ehhhhhh, ughhhhhh. Ehhhhhh, ughhhhhh," completing in his mind the funny picture of *Dingbat*, all arms and legs awkwardly in motion.

"Sally is doing her best," said Perfect.

"Oh, yeah. Sure she is," Elliot thought.

Perfect said, "No one likes her, and she knows it. But I like her."

Elliot stood still for a moment. "Oh. Of course you do. I'm sorry to have done that, Perfect. Is there something you want to do?"

"No, Elliot. Not now, at least. I simply want you to be aware of how fear would affect you, keeping you distant from Sally and distracted from me. That was fear's suggested reaction—mockery—not yours. I interrupted so you may know me today, and how different things will be. I am patient with Sally and will do much with her. There is more to her than you know."

"I never ... I never thought like that, Perfect. I am glad to know that, and I trust what you know and will do. Let's go to school, Perfect."

Elliot walked through the schoolhouse door held open by the ever sun-beaming Miss Breckett, only to bump into Nancy Eaton —*again*. A furious storm blew up on her face, and she whispered angrily, "Samuelson! Why must you bump me so much? And where's my three dollars?"

All Elliot could get out was, "Ahh, umm, well . . ." Nancy slapped her hands on her hips and glowered at a defenseless Elliot.

"Perfect," Elliot thought, "what now?"

He replied, "Apologize and tell her that you don't have it, and that she might as well do what she's going to do."

An avalanche of protest presented itself in Elliot's mind. Elliot knew that it was dangerous to fall into the punishing hands of the Eaton family. But to purposefully throw himself in, when an excuse could delay certain pain? Unacceptable. Irresponsible. "DON'T DO IT," he thought.

"I am patient with Nancy," said Perfect. "Trust me—I am with you —and you will be patient in what I will do."

Before he could give "DON'T DO IT" any more attention, Elliot said softly, "Ah, I'm sorry for bumping into you again, Nancy. I don't have three dollars, so you, um, might as well do what you've got to do."

Nancy hissed, "Well that's great, Samuelson. I'll see you at lunch . . . with my brothers." With an indignant shake of her head, she turned and marched away.

"You have not followed fear," said Perfect immediately, "because you know me, Elliot, and I am doing something with you about Nancy. Patience in expectation will very soon help her. Well done."

Walking to his seat, Elliot was transfixed by what he knew and felt; he was with Perfect, who was unmoved by the fear Elliot felt. Perfect was his hope against fear, which was right then cluttering Elliot's mind with nervous thoughts about how to avoid imminent doom brought on by his refusal to change course away from Perfect's direction.

"Fear, shut up!" commanded Elliot. "Perfect and I have a lot to do together, and he is patient, so I am too."

18

KINDNESS

"Good morning, class!" said Miss Breckett cheerily. "Aren't you glad to be here, where learning is so fun? Who wouldn't want to be here, especially when it's time for arithmetic?"

Elliot stifled a groan. He knew better than to be honest, particularly when Miss Breckett wanted compliance, decorated with smiles.

"Perfect," thought Elliot, "why is it so difficult for me to be here? I feel so stupid—I've never told anyone that—especially about arithmetic. But I have to pretend that I like it."

Before there could be an answer, Dan Westerly whispered, "Oh, boy; Samuelson's favorite subject—to be stupid."

Elliot quickly looked at Dan, and while preparing to load up a defensive insult, paused just long enough to pay attention to the struggle in his mind. Anger announced itself to him and demanded punishment for Dan, inducing Elliot to clench his teeth and fists.

"Elliot," said Perfect, "I know Dan. He's an awful nuisance, but one that I will soon meet in kindness."

Caught between two forces, Elliot thought, "Perfect, what am I to do? I've got to do something."

"Do you?" asked Perfect. "Dan is troubled and lonely, but you're not. You are well with me."

And anger fizzled.

In its place was Perfect—and his kindness toward Dan. With barely a thought, Elliot said quietly to Dan, "You're right. Arithmetic makes me feel stupid. I don't like it."

The ogre-like look on Dan's face vanished, replaced by an uncommonly blank stare. For the first time, there was no verbal poison served in Dan's response. "Oh. Yeah. Me, too," was all he said.

"I can't believe I told Dan Westerly the truth," thought Elliot. "He's the last person . . ."

"That you'd want to do that with, I know," interjected Perfect. "Consider the anger that you felt, Elliot. Anger is a cousin of fear, and together they would induce you to live barricaded from people, as though that were the wisest option. But I am the wisest option, as you know. Dan will never again be the same toward you, nor will you be toward him. You and I have given him an undeserved kindness that has startled him to a beginning . . . a beginning I will continue."

Deeply focused, Elliot thought, "That was something I would never normally do, but, it felt, well, *real.* More real than anything ever. Like I'm alive for the first time. Does that make sense, Perfect?"

"Yes, because you are. Heads up, now."

"Who would like to solve a problem on our new blackboard?" Miss Breckett asked. Donna Jensen shot her hand heavenward and was immediately favored by Miss Breckett. "Why, yes!" she said, exuding delight. "Miss Jensen is our best at arithmetic, and aren't we pleased, class, that she has volunteered? Of course, we are!"

Elliot thought just the opposite, and was darkened in his thinking. "No, we're sick of Donna. We *hate* Donna and wish she'd go away."

As Donna walked to the blackboard to solve the problem written there, Elliot thought how lucky she was to be so good at arithmetic. Her strength made his unfortunate weakness all the more glaring, and he scowled at her as she paraded her way forward. "I hate you," he thought.

"No, you don't," said Perfect.

"Yes, I do," thought Elliot. "She makes me sick."

Donna began working out the equation with evident glee, and in a few moments, announced, "There you are—the answer is one hundred and eighty-one!"

Elliot, still dark and brooding, didn't notice that Miss Breckett did not share in Donna's exuberance. The room grew tense as, one by one, Donna's classmates realized that all was not well. Something was wrong.

"Is there anything someone might want to change about Miss Jensen's answer?" asked a less than enthused, but still smiling Miss Breckett. No one moved. It felt like no one breathed, including a suddenly confused Donna.

Her face, now tight and ashen, revealed the fear Donna knew at the blackboard. Her eyes darted from Miss Breckett to her classmates and back again, until finally riveting upon the comparative safety of the floor.

"Fear is hurting Donna," said Perfect. "You can see its work evidenced in her eyes. What do you think about that, Elliot?"

"Well, she, um, ah . . . I don't like fear when it bothers me. I guess I don't I like it for Donna, either."

Miss Breckett, feeling the darkness for too long, sun-beamed to the blackboard and said, "Well, class, Miss Jensen is oh-so close, but made one tragic mistake." Chalk in hand, Miss Breckett always wrote as if she were a ballerina—gracefully flowing from left to right and back again, with exaggerated movements befitting the elegant dance. "Sixteen times thirteen, minus twenty-five is not one hundred and eighty-one, but one hundred and eighty-three." She wrote the correct answer. "Can you see, class? Can you see where Miss Jensen made her mistake? Of course you can. Alright, Miss Jensen, you may return to your seat. I'm certain you will do better next time."

"Donna is right now thinking that there will never be a 'next time,'" said Perfect. "Because she has been so good at arithmetic, failure is a heavy shame that fear is now speaking to her. We're going to do something for Donna."

"Wow," thought Elliot. "You weren't kidding when you said that this is your day at school."

Perfect asked, "You noticed an argument in your mind, didn't you, Elliot? Fear has a big mouth, and it gave you thoughts and words of jealousy. Do you remember?"

"I, um, yes, I do."

"Fear even gave you words of hatred toward Donna, something that has nothing to do with you nor me. That is from fear and not from you, even though you felt it."

"I did feel it," said Elliot. "Fear is sneaky. It said '*I hate you*,' and I followed along with it so much so that I didn't recognize and talk with you when you said '*No, you don't.*' You were trying to rescue me, weren't you, Perfect?"

"Yes, I was. This is also school for you today . . . and every day, really, since I love being with you and being who I am against fear. Remember this, Elliot: I am Perfect, so you don't have to be."

Elliot's eyes suddenly moved to Donna, and held her closely there, just as he had with his mother in the garden.

"Say what comes to mind now," said Perfect. "It will feel like you because it will be us together."

"Donna," said Elliot, loudly enough for everyone to hear. "You're still the best we've got." Everyone turned immediately to Elliot, including a big-eyed Miss Breckett.

Before she could get a word out, Donna, her fallen face suddenly lifted in surprise, said, "Thank you. Thank you, Elliot."

A chorus of murmured agreement filled the classroom.

19

GOODNESS

"Why not sit next to Don?" asked Perfect. It was lunchtime, and that meant a quick and vital assessment of people and groups so Elliot could choose where best to sit. He didn't like conflict—not at all—and had learned how to position himself strategically in order to avoid it. Mostly. Sort of. Not really, but he still tried.

So when Perfect asked the question, plenty of reasons not to sit next to Don came immediately to mind. "He is the biggest bully I know!" thought Elliot. "I'm scared to sit next to him."

"Yes, I know," said Perfect, calmly. "That might ordinarily be wise, but not today because I am going to free you from fear when facing Don. This is how we walk together—I am Perfect, and you are growing confident about me with you, and about me with others. Let's offer him the carrot in your lunch."

Feeling both fear and excitement, Elliot walked to where Don was seated at a playground table.

"What do you want, Samuelson?" asked a bothered Nibecker, his face pinched in cynicism.

"Well, ah, I'm going to sit here. You want a carrot?"

"*Really*? You're offering me your carrot? Why?"

Fear began to fade as Perfect secured Elliot, and peace over-whelmed insecurity. Sitting down and reaching into his lunch pail, Elliot held out the carrot, laughed and said, "I don't know. I guess you're going to get it anyway, so I'm offering a shortcut." In the silence that followed, anything could have happened, which is why Elliot was keenly aware of a rumble-jumble of feelings and thoughts: "*Danger! Now anything could happen, you idiot!*'

"Well, okay then," said Don. "I'll take it. But I'll bet it would taste better if I'd stolen it like I usually do." He laughed.

"You might be right," agreed Elliot. "But at least I don't have to be surprised by that happy, mouth-full-of-food smile of yours."

Don crunched on the carrot. "Well, I can still show that to you. *Ahhhhhhh*," he said, opening wide his orange-loaded mouth.

"Oh, great, Nibecker!" said Elliot, with a smile.

"What are you two fools doing?" asked Donna. "I thought I'd better get over here before one of you smacked the other." She sat down at the table. "Hey, Sally! Elliot just gave some of his lunch to Don. Why not sit over here so you can watch these fools?"

Momentarily surprised, Sally quickly corrected her face, and acted like she was often invited to sit with people. "Well, um, okay. Why not?"

Nothing like this had ever happened, and no one knew what to do or what was to come.

Elliot, while doing his best to appear calm, was anything but. He had a long history of fearing Don and of not liking know-it-all Donna or Dingbat Sally. Yet here he was, surrounded. "Perfect," he thought, "what are you doing? This is crazy."

"You would have been right a few days ago, Elliot," said Perfect, "but now that I'm here with you, everything is new, and you are not subject to fear's way of hiding, but my way of freedom. Offer Sally a piece of your bread."

"Am I going to have any lunch at all?" Elliot thought as he reached for it.

"Because you and I are together and you're not hiding in fear, this will be your best lunch ever . . . so far. Watch what I will bring about with you."

"Sally," asked Elliot, "would you like a piece of my bread?" All three heads turned toward him, as if he had asked something profoundly unknowable. None of them had ever been open to any of the others, only guarded and combative, as was common in Sarx. Each had learned to pre-navigate around the pain of asking a question that might result in rejection, or worse, ridicule. But Elliot's offer threw them into navigational chaos.

"That's it, Elliot," said Perfect. "Well done."

"How did you know I didn't have any today?" asked Sally. "My good-for-nothing brother ate it all before school. So, yes, I would, actually."

Elliot tore off half of his and handed it toward her. Immediately, Don lunged forward, grabbed the bread, and took a large and happy bite out of it before handing it on to a dumbfounded Sally.

"Eeeeooooow, Don!" she exclaimed, "that's gross!"

"I know!" said Don, excitedly chewing on the stolen bread. "How does it look?" he asked, opening wide his bread-stuffed mouth for Sally to see.

"Eeeeooooow," she exclaimed. "Keep it to yourself!" Sally's disapproving brow could not hide that she was smiling.

"See?" laughed Donna. "I told you they were fools."

As fascinating as it all was, Elliot was more aware of the peace he knew than he was of the dangerous exchange at the table. "Perfect," he thought, "is this what life is like with you?"

"Yes, it is," he answered. "I am life with you, Elliot. What you and I know and do together affects every day."

"But that was good of you, Samuelson," said Donna, who suddenly turned thoughtful. "And thank you for saving me in class. I've never been so ashamed in all my life."

"Well, what he said is true, Donna," said Sally. "You are the best at arithmetic. Everybody knows. Didn't you hear us agree with Elliot?"

"She's right," Don said.

"I guess so," Donna answered. Her voice softened. "I've just never made a mistake like that, you know, in front of everyone, and I didn't know what to do. It felt awful."

"Donna is brave," said Perfect. Elliot knew it was true. "Why not tell her now?" Perfect asked.

"In front of them?" thought Elliot. "Now? But then she'll . . . they'll . . ." He was immediately stuck because he was used to hiding from others by keeping to himself words that revealed what he really thought. Elliot trusted his inner barricade. Going ahead with Perfect's leading would take him into the open again—defenseless. It was risky and uncertain. "I can't do it," thought Elliot, and fear filled his feelings, influencing him to the easier course of silence. He bit into his bread.

"I am here with you," said Perfect.

"*Okay, okay*," thought Elliot, nervously.

"Remember, my friend," said Perfect, "you don't have to say or do anything I tell you, but you are finding that as you do, you are better for it."

Of course, Perfect was right. As Elliot thought about the truth of it, fear backed away, and he knew the way forward.

"Look, Donna," he said, "you are brave. I wouldn't do what you did. I'm too scared."

"Brave?" asked Donna. "Me?"

"Yes, you," added Sally.

"I've always thought so, too," said Don.

"But I was terrified," Donna replied, "especially of Miss Breckett and what she might do to me. How is that brave?"

"I don't think having fear means you're not brave," said Elliot, who was surprised by how easily it came out of his mouth.

"Well, I sure didn't feel brave," said Donna.

Just then, Elliot noticed a downcast Nancy Eaton sauntering past, her eyes avoiding those at the table.

"Nancy believes that something is wrong, but I am doing something right," said Perfect.

"Even for her?" asked Elliot.

Perfect laughed. "Yes, my friend, even for her. Let's do the unexpected and ask her to join you at the table. There's room."

"But that's crazy, Perfect!" thought Elliot. "Are you sure?" But he heard nothing in response.

Nancy's pace had already taken her past the table, and Elliot could feel the moment slipping away. "Um ... um ... Nancy," he muttered, not loudly enough to be heard. "Nancy," he said again, to no affect. "NANCY!" he yelled, and got her attention.

She stopped, turned her head and asked, "*What*? What is it, Samuelson?"

Elliot was super aware—of how this felt, of how it looked, and of how crazy it was to ask someone as unfriendly as Nancy Eaton to do anything, let alone something together. "Well," he thought, "I have nothing to lose since Perfect is here with me and it's his day." A genuine smile crossed his face and Elliot was filled joy. "I don't know what's going to happen," he thought, "but here goes."

"Wanna sit with us?" he asked.

Again, time seemed to stop around him, while competing thoughts of fear and hope bashed about his mind.

"Did you already talk to Tad or Tom?" Nancy asked, her eyes squinting in suspicion.

"No," answered Elliot. "Why would I do that?"

"Because they just told me to fight my own fights, and they're not going to help me with you."

"Well, that's good news,' thought Elliot.

"Mm-hmm," said Perfect.

Elliot suppressed a smile at this turn of events. "Well, why not sit with us then?"

"Forget it, Samuelson," Nancy said bitterly. "I'm not sitting with you and your gang."

"Why not, Nancy?" asked Don. "We won't bite. Well, *they* won't bite, but I might—especially if you've got something good in your lunch pail."

"Well ..." Nancy's face softened. "All right. But no lunch for you, Nibecker!"

And Nancy joined them.

20

FAITHFULNESS

That afternoon, when leaving school, Elliot turned right, thinking that he'd like to go see what was left of the church building after the fire. His day with Perfect had been amazing, especially lunch. He had never ever talked with so many of his classmates except in argument. Although they fumbled their way through conversation at the table, each expressed that they wanted to have lunch together again the next day—especially if Elliot promised to share his.

Perfect and Elliot had given much of Elliot's lunch away, and he was hungry. While he didn't have three dollars, he did have 25 cents, so he hoped to find something to eat by stopping at Mrs. Westerly's store.

"Elliot," said Perfect, "what did you think of our day at school?"

"Well, you must know," Elliot replied. "You were there."

"Of course. But I enjoy talking with you. Assumptions about what I know could cause less conversation, less understanding and more confusion for you as a result. And that's when fear gets busy. I don't want that for you, Elliot."

"Oh! You're right," Elliot said. "What was I thinking? I love talking with you, Perfect. How could I say something so dumb?"

"You will never, ever be dumb, Elliot. It's just that old ways of avoiding conversations that might be difficult are now being challenged by this new way with me—this way with me that you enjoy so much. You are new, Elliot, and so is this. What did you think of Nancy accepting our invitation?"

"I didn't know what to think, Perfect! All I knew was that, because I trust you, I asked her, despite the reasons I had for *not* asking her. I know I've said it before, but I felt so alive in doing it. This is life now, isn't it, Perfect?"

"Yes, this is. This is life with me, Elliot."

"And how, or maybe *why*, did Tad and Tom Eaton decide to not help Nancy, when they always have before? At least, as far as I know."

Perfect answered, "What do you think happened?"

"I don't know!" thought Elliot, "except I think you had something to do with it. Did you, Perfect?"

Perfect laughed. "There is much that I am doing, as you now know. I am busy. There will be times when I tell you what I am doing and thinking about others, but the security—the hope—that you have is because of where I am and what I am doing with you. I am and will always be faithful to you, Elliot. I think you know that. Do you realize that my faithfulness to you worked out in how you were faithful with Donna, Don, Sally and Nancy? Despite the challenges from fear and the long history you have with it, you focused upon me. Well done."

"Oh, Perfect," exclaimed Elliot, "I love you and how you are with me! And I think that's how you'd be with them. Is that right?"

"Can you imagine me being any other way?" answered Perfect. "No, you cannot. This is why I love doing everything with you, Elliot, so that you know me and what I am like. I will never ask you to do anything, except we do it together and know each other through it. Now, how about a piece of jerky from Mrs. Westerly?"

Stepping into the store, Elliot walked toward where he knew Mrs. Westerly kept the dried meat. But before he got there, as he rounded a corner, he collided with Miss Breckett and both fell awkwardly to the floor. As Elliot gathered himself, Perfect said, "She is despairing, and I will help her."

"Mr. Samuelson," she said, "I'm so sorry."

"Oh, no, Miss Breckett. It was my fault. I bump into people all the time."

Standing now, Miss Breckett turned to Elliot, who could immediately see the tears on her face. She wiped them away as quickly as she could.

"I meant that I'm sorry you had to see me like this," she said, "crying and all. It's really nothing, nothing at all. I will be just fine in a moment, I assure you."

"I cry, Miss Breckett—sometimes because I'm happy, but usually because I'm sad," replied Elliot. "Which one is this?"

Elliot was aware of how easily he asked the question, but especially of how little he feared Miss Breckett. Elliot knew that Perfect was with him, and he cared for her more than he feared her.

"Listen to her," said Perfect.

As Elliot thought about what Perfect said, Miss Breckett fixed her hair and dress, and began folding a piece of paper before putting it quickly into her bag.

"Well," she said, smiling, "it all depends upon how one looks at it.

One can choose to be sad, or one can choose to be happy. In no time at all, I shall be happy." As Elliot kept his eyes to hers and said nothing more, Miss Breckett wavered, sobbed and broke into tears. Reaching for a handkerchief, she applied it to her face as much to hide as to catch the wet. "I'm sorry," she cried, "I'm so sorry for you to see me like this. It's inexcusable, really. What must you think of me, Mr. Samuelson? Please give me a moment, and I will be fine. Really, I will."

"She's not fine," said Perfect. Elliot suddenly knew that Miss Breckett was not the woman he had thought she was. Strangely, he was glad for it . . . and relieved. "Say what you're thinking, Elliot," said Perfect.

Calmly, Elliot said, "Well, Miss Breckett, whichever these are, happy or sad, crying is okay. I don't mind seeing tears, and I won't tell anyone."

"That's it," said Perfect.

With that, Miss Breckett wailed loudly, and Elliot drew nearer to support her in any way he could. Hearing the turmoil, Mrs. Westerly moved from behind the counter and motioned for Elliot to step back so she could move in to keep Miss Breckett from falling.

"This is just right," said Perfect.

"*It is?*" thought Elliot. "It seems awful."

"For Miss Breckett, this is a beginning," said Perfect. "She has long endured a dark fatigue that she can no longer hide with a smile and sunny disposition. She is exhausted because pretended sunshine has no strength and no warmth."

"Oh," said Elliot. "I didn't know . . . I didn't . . . um . . . I thought . . ."

"You couldn't have known because it was not for you to know without me," said Perfect. "I alone know what keeps people to fear in secret. And I alone am their freedom. Do you understand this, Elliot?"

"I think so. Perfect, you are why I was not afraid just now. You are why I saw Miss Breckett as I never have, and you are why I cared about her—even drew near to her, when I never would have without you."

"Yes, I am," said Perfect. "And because of how I am with you, Miss Breckett knew that you were faithful to protect her—even to keep her presumed shame a secret. This is how we are, Elliot. This is what we do, you and I, because we are together and you are knowing me."

Just then, Dan Westerly came from the other side of the store. "Wow. Miss Breckett sure is a mess. I never thought I'd see her like this."

"Me neither," Elliot replied, "but I'm glad. There's more to her than we thought. I think your mother's going to help her."

They watched as Mrs. Westerly hugged and helped Miss Breckett to a chair in the adjacent office behind the counter and began calmly soothing her.

"I guess I'll watch the store for now," said Dan. "Samuelson, do you want a piece of jerky? No charge today."

"I sure would," Elliot replied.

21
———

MEEKNESS

E lliot left the store and walked toward the rubble that was now the church. "Perfect," he thought, "I know I've already said this, but I'm convinced that everything that's best is with you. And everything else is best understood as I know you. Every day I want to be aware of you, so that everything that happens around me fits into life with you. No matter what, I'm okay because you're with me."

"And that's life, Elliot," replied Perfect. "You are just right with me, and what happens around you—including Reverend Fortner—is always something I'm involved in with you. Reverend Fortner is just ahead, and will have something to say to you. Do not let fear distract you, but look for me, and you will be well."

"I will do my best, Perfect, but I am already afraid of that man," Elliot admitted.

"And not without reason, I know. But as you have seen, not all of the feelings you feel are from you, let alone from me. Feelings such as anger, envy and hatred are not simply things to be avoided, but indicators, and are best understood by knowing me, even as you feel them. In that way they get your attention, but not your submission."

"I think I'm learning that, Perfect, and it's quite a change for me— one that makes everything new. So is it okay if I don't have much to say with Reverend Fortner? If I just wait until he's done, and then leave? I really don't want to be around him for long."

"Yes, it is, Elliot," said Perfect. "But silence will not always be what's best for us. People want to know what to say and do beforehand so they can control what hasn't yet happened. That can become a dangerous temptation. Navigating the moments of life separate from me is not possible, and cheats those who make the attempt. I am what everyone needs in every circumstance. You and I are together, and nothing can overtake us or separate us, no matter what . . . or *who*. Look for me, Elliot, and you will have what you need."

"I will, Perfect," said Elliot.

Reverend Fortner, loaded with more power and personality than a circus, rose from where he had been seated at the side of the rubble and began walking toward Elliot.

"Mr. Samuelson!" he bellowed, "Have you come to claim responsi-bility for the destruction of the house of the Lord?" Reverend Fortner squinted and lowered his head toward Elliot to thoroughly examine his suspect.

Perfect said, "Reverend Fortner believes that the only way for good to happen is for everyone's secrets to be exposed, except his own. He has confused prosecution and accomplishment with living, and he is alone because of it. Few people come close to those who only want to use them."

"Well, that's a big problem," thought Elliot. "I wonder if a lot of us do that."

Perfect replied, "Elliot, I do not expose; I cover and protect. Tell the Reverend, 'I have nothing to claim, but I wonder if I might be of help to you.'"

Even as fear immediately began to protest ("I don't ever want to be anywhere near him!"), Elliot did exactly as Perfect said, and then told fear, "You are not my friend, fear, and I do not trust you."

"Well done, Elliot," said Perfect.

Reverend Fortner drew a long breath. "No one has come forward to confess this deed. How can I build a church if people can't be trusted?" he asked, gazing out over Sarx. "Have they no fear of God?"

"Well," replied Elliot, "I don't know about them, but here I am."

A refocused Reverend Fortner looked back at Elliot, and asked, "And why should I trust you, Mr. Samuelson? I don't know you or your family, but I think you're guilty of plenty of things. Have you confessed? You're not part of my church, and you're just a boy."

Perfect said, "What he says is true, although it says more about him than you, Elliot. Agree with him and offer to help clean up."

"That's true," said Elliot. "But, um . . ." Elliot rarely offered to help someone, mostly because it was more of a duty than a desire. All of his chores at home were responsibilities—work that had to be done or a penalty awaited. Elliot did what he had to do because it was expected of him. Judgment followed if he failed. Actually, judgment followed no matter what he did, and he was tired of feeling measured. Nevertheless, he said, "I don't know if I'm trustworthy, Reverend Fortner. But I'll help clean up."

Just then, Mrs. Boyer happened upon them. Elliot hadn't seen her since he had delivered the eggs to her house. With a quick yank of her face that brought up all of the bitterness she could muster, she screeched, "I'd be done with that Samuelson boy, if I were you, Reverend. Neither he nor his family are to be trusted."

Elliot felt overwhelmed by ridicule, and heard in his mind, "For some lousy eggs? How dare she be so rude. What does she know about anything? I should tell her off right now. Rude? She's never seen rude like I can do rude."

"You are well," said Perfect.

Caught between fear and Perfect, Elliot thought, "I don't know what's right at this moment, except I know Perfect. He is right, and I am well with him." Elliot, refusing fear's suggested course, had nothing to say. He looked away from Mrs. Boyer to Reverend Fortner and back again, and still he had nothing to say. It just wasn't in him.

"You are well," said Perfect.

"I believe you," thought Elliot. And he did. And he was. No one said anything. They just looked at each other—Mrs. Boyer's bitter-twisted face, Reverend Fortner's guilt-giving stare, and Elliot's defenseless calm.

Mrs. Boyer was first to crack. "Well, maybe give him a broom, Reverend, but keep an eye on him! Good thing there's nothing to steal, I'd say."

As she began to amble off, bitter face and all, Elliot looked anew at her and found compassion welling up inside. "It's very hard to be Mrs. Boyer, isn't it, Perfect?" he thought.

"I wish you well, Mrs. Boyer!" Elliot said.

Mrs. Boyer jerked to a stop, turned toward Elliot, and with a jab of her cane, said, "I doubt that. You Samuelsons always want something from me, but I'm not fooled. Not now, not ever." With that, she turned and stormed off.

"Why doesn't anybody trust me?" thought Elliot.

"I do," said Perfect, "and I know you meant what you said. Mrs. Boyer has a problem, but you're not the problem."

As the Reverend and Elliot watched her walk away, Elliot thought, "But I wish that could have gone better. She's so sad."

"Yes, she is," said Perfect, "But you are not responsible for her happiness, Elliot. That is ahead of her, but not now."

Reverend Fortner, unaccustomed to being on the far edge of attention, said, "Well then, Mr. Samuelson. Perhaps a broom is a first step toward proving your trustworthiness to me."

"Ask him why that's important, Elliot," Perfect said.

When Elliot calmly did so, Reverend Fortner was surprised, and made sure to show it. "Well, young man, if you're going to become part of this church, we've got to know if you're worthy of our trust. Otherwise we will hold you in suspicion—maybe even of starting this fire. Is that what you want, Mr. Samuelson?"

Elliot paused to think, and replied, "I don't know how the fire started, Reverend Fortner. But I know someone who says I'm trustworthy. I will help you because he trusts me, and that's enough for me. Where would you like me to start?"

22

SELF-CONTROL

Fortunately, Elliot could no longer smell smoke. He had swept ash and moved half-burned wood for long enough that he'd grown used to the smell. That didn't mean anyone else missed the odor hanging upon him, and his soot-covered clothing induced everyone to avoid him as he began to walk home—everyone except Mrs. Westerly, who crossed the road to reach him, her gait purposeful and face kindly toward Elliot.

"Oh, Mr. Samuelson! Elliot?" she called.

"Yes, Mrs. Westerly?"

"A word with you, please," she said.

Adults rarely, if ever, sought out a boy like Elliot because people were suspicious of outside-of-the-family contacts. Naturally, this made Elliot concerned. "Perfect? Am I in trouble?"

"You are not. Not at all. Let's enjoy this."

Looking directly into Elliot's eyes, Mrs. Westerly said, "I want to thank you for what you did in my store today. I have never seen anyone treat Miss Breckett with such care as you did. What got into you, boy?"

"Well, I saw how troubled she was, and, um, I just cared." Elliot paused for a moment to look for Perfect.

"You are well, Elliot. You needn't say much. This is for listening."

"Well, Elliot," Mrs. Westerly commented, "you cared beautifully. What you could not have known was that Miss Breckett had just read a telegram that her father had died suddenly. You were the first person to see her after getting the news, and she was terribly undone. I know what the death of someone close, someone important, someone you love does to a person, but I could not have done what you did."

Peace and love filled Elliot, and tears spilled out as evidence, as Perfect made himself known to him.

"I know what Miss Breckett is like," said Mrs. Westerly. "Most of us avoid her if we can, and Dan has told me what she can be like as a teacher. But there you stood, unmoved by fear in the moment. You showed great self-control, Elliot, and I was moved to help Miss Breckett because I saw you. I came to my senses because of you—I recognized grief like mine—and that is why I cared for her as I did. I told her about my husband's death and what it meant to me, and I've never told anyone about that. She and I have much more to say to each other, because we've begun a friendship that we never would have except for her obvious sorrow and your care. I can't thank you enough, young man."

Without the slightest hesitation, Mrs. Westerly nearly smothered Elliot with a giant hug. "Thank you, dear boy, thank you," she said, her voice a quavering whisper.

Elliot wasn't sure what to say. "You're ... welcome, Mrs. Westerly."

After a few moments, Mrs. Westerly released her grip and stood back. She looked ghastly, with Elliot's soot and ash now painting her face and clothing, the result of clean meeting dirty. But neither of them cared, since both were better by far for the meeting.

"This is the way of life, Elliot, where you and I meet people and rub off on them, and they on us," said Perfect.

Elliot laughed aloud while looking at Mrs. Westerly, mostly because he understood Perfect's meaning. "I've made a mess of you, Mrs. Westerly."

"I haven't a care about that, Elliot. That was the best, most important hug I've given in a long time. And, yes—it turned out to be the smelliest, too! I think I will never forget it." Wiping the ash from her tear-streaked face, Mrs. Westerly turned to go.

"Thank you for telling me, Mrs. Westerly. I have never really known Miss Breckett until today, and I think I've never really known you, either. But I'm sure glad I do now."

She turned back toward Elliot and said with a big smile, "I am, too." And with a laugh strong and bold, she said, "We could sure use more of this in Sarx! I'm hopeful because of you. See you soon, Elliot."

As Mrs. Westerly headed back to her store, Elliot thought, "Well, that was wonderful, Perfect. And I did so little for so much."

"It was," Perfect replied, "but the little you and I did together has been entirely uncommon for the people of Sarx. I am what they need, Elliot. Together as we are, we give them some of me each day."

As Elliot began to move toward home, he thought, "Perfect, everything I've ever wanted—even more than I knew I wanted—is with you. Even with Miss Breckett and Reverend Fortner, when I once would have known and followed fear—as if it were best—you kept me from it. And when Mrs. Westerly said I had great self-control, I know it was because you are that for me. You've made me alive, Perfect." Once again, Elliot was filled with joy.

"It's true," Perfect replied. "I am life. With me you lack nothing, and have more than you could dream. Many are confused about self-control, believing that it originates with themselves. They think they must keep themselves from being bad. It's restricting, they believe. But you have found that self-control is with me—right here —and that it holds you to the good that you now are. It's a freedom and a release of what we are together."

Rounding a corner that brought the Buffalo River into view, Elliot could not help but shout, "You are perfect, Perfect!"

"I am!" shouted Perfect in response. "How about inviting Don Nibecker for a swim in the river one day after school? I think he would like a swim, especially the way you do it, Elliot."

"I think you're right," said Elliot. "I'll ask him if he can swim."

"He can," answered Perfect, "and I am beginning to meet with him, as I did with you."

With a gasp, Elliot asked, "You are? *With Don*? Wow."

"Yes, with Don. I am happy to be getting his attention. Do you think he will like me, Elliot?"

"Are you kidding, Perfect?" asked Elliot. "There is nothing I could want more than for Don to meet you. Nothing. I know that only you could arrange for that, so I am happy to do anything to help. You will be perfect for Don."

"Yes, Elliot. I will be. He has already asked for my name."

"What did you tell him?"

"Same as I told you. My name is Perfect."

"Did he ask how you got that name?"

"Yes, he did, Elliot. And I told him much the same as I told you: 'You'll see. I will show you.'"

As they reached Dornan' corner, Perfect asked, "How about a swim, Elliot?"

"Do you like to swim, Perfect?" Elliot asked. "I had no idea."

"Are you kidding? I love heights and I love water," said Perfect. "Race you to the bottom!"

"But how can we race? You're in me. We're together, Perfect."

"Oh yeah." Perfect laughed. "That's right. I wonder how far and deep we can get together?"

"Farther and deeper than ever!" shouted Elliot.

"Ready! Set! Go!" said Perfect and Elliot in unison, as they launched down the hillside.

"Woo-hoo!" they yelled. "Woo-hooooo!"

Indeed. Farther and deeper than ever.

ALSO BY RALPH HARRIS

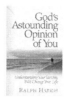

God's Astounding Opinion of You

Understanding Your Identity Will Change Your Life

Many people would be surprised to learn that God's view of them is much greater and positive than their own. Ralph Harris leads readers to experience a deeply satisfying, joyful relationship with Christ as they embrace what God thinks of them—that they are holy, righteous, blameless, and lovable.

With beautifully communicated biblical knowledge and examples of God's grace, Harris turns readers toward the love affair with God they were made for. Revealing and unique insights help readers:

- exchange fear and obligation for delight and devotion

- recognize the remarkable role and strength of the Holy Spirit in their daily lives

- view their identity—a new creation—as the new normal, and live accordingly!

Readers will encounter wisdom, direction, and encouragement as they rest in God's truth and grace, develop a sincere partnership with Christ, and live as confident children of God.

ABOUT THE AUTHOR

~

Ralph Harris has been a pastor and teacher to children, youth and adults for more than 35 years. He is marked by depth, authenticity and playfulness, which combine for safe and freeing environments that lead to genuine and trusting relationships in which Jesus can be more easily known and enjoyed. That's his passion. He is the best-selling author of God's Astounding Opinion of You, and is now a well-traveled speaker who writes extensively and posts encouraging video messages at RalphHarris.org. He and his wife, Sarah, live in Longmont, Colorado, while their daughters, Ellen and Emma, are led by the grace and love of God from Montana to New Zealand—and places in between.

If you've enjoyed getting to know Elliot and Perfect, and maybe yourself a little better, too, Ralph would love to connect with you.

facebook.com/ralphharris

twitter.com/RalphHa97434568

instagram.com/therever

Made in the USA
Lexington, KY
07 December 2019